OURS TO TELL
RECLAIMING INDIGENOUS STORIES

annick press
toronto • berkeley

ELDON YELLOWHORN
KATHY LOWINGER

© 2025 Eldon Yellowhorn (text)
© 2025 Kathy Lowinger (text)

Cover art: Chantal Jung
Interior art (pages 5, 6, 9, 127, 130, 134): Chantal Jung
Interior art (pages 13, 75): Coco Apunnguaq Lynge
Cover designed by Sam Tse
Interior designed by Sam Tse

Edited by Rachel Taylor
Photo research by Mary Rose MacLachlan
Copy edited by Lisa Frenette
Proofread by Linda Pruessen
Index by Rhiannon Thomas

Acknowledgment
With thanks to Rivka Cranley for her diligent work. —K. L.

Annick Press Ltd.
All rights reserved. No part of this work covered by the copyrights hereon may be reproduced or used in any form or by any means—graphic, electronic, or mechanical—without the prior written permission of the publisher.

Cover Credits

Background: Memorial University of Newfoundland. Libraries. Centre for Newfoundland Studies; flower panels: Courtesy of Elias Jade Not Afraid.

Collage by Chantal Jung: Courtesy of Jay Odjick; Charles S. Cochran, photo, Vancouver Public Library 9430; National Anthropological Archives, Smithsonian Institution; Photo by Latoya Flowers; Photo by George Paul; Courtesy of Agnes Yellow Bear. Frame © rawpixel, Freepik.com.

Interior image credits continued on page 130

 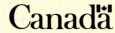

This book is funded in part by the Government of Canada. *Ce livre est financé en partie par le gouvernement du Canada.* We acknowledge the support of the Canada Council for the Arts. *Nous remercions le Conseil des arts du Canada de son soutien.* We would like to acknowledge the funding support of the Ontario Arts Council (OAC) and the Government of Ontario for their support. We also acknowledge the support of the Government of Ontario through the Ontario Book Publishing Tax Credit, and through Ontario Creates.

Library and Archives Canada Cataloguing in Publication

Title: Ours to tell : reclaiming Indigenous stories / written by Eldon Yellowhorn and Kathy Lowinger.
Names: Yellowhorn, Eldon, 1956- author | Lowinger, Kathy, author
Description: Includes bibliographical references and index.
Identifiers: Canadiana (print) 20240416996 | Canadiana (ebook) 20240417054 | ISBN 9781773219530 (hardcover) | ISBN 9781773219547 (softcover) | ISBN 9781773219554 (EPUB) | ISBN 9781773219561 (PDF)
Subjects: LCSH: Indigenous peoples—Canada—Biography—Juvenile literature. | LCSH: Indigenous authors—Canada—Biography—Juvenile literature. | CSH: Indigenous artists—Canada—Biography—Juvenile literature. | LCGFT: Biographies.
Classification: LCC E89 .Y45 2025 | DDC j971.004/9700922—dc23

Published in the U.S.A. by Annick Press (U.S.) Ltd.
Distributed in Canada by University of Toronto Press.
Distributed in the U.S.A. by Publishers Group West.

Printed in China

annickpress.com

Also available as an e-book. Please visit annickpress.com/ebooks for more details.

In memory of Pat Malis, a splendid reader, poet, and sister

—K. L.

For my Kaitlin

—E. Y.

TABLE OF CONTENTS

A Note about Language and Terms   7
Introduction: Ours to Tell   8

Part 1: We Tell Our Story in Images and Symbols   11

Chapter 1: Gaspar Antonio Chi: Rebel Scribe   13
Maya

Chapter 2: Sequoyah Invents a Syllabary   19
Cherokee

Part 2: We Report the Story   23

Chapter 3: Elias Boudinot's Story Was a Warning   25
Cherokee

Chapter 4: Ella Cara Deloria's Insider Story   31
Yankton Sioux

Part 3: Our History Is in Our Poems, Songs, and Written Stories   39

Chapter 5: Pauline Johnson: Poet Pop Star   41
Mohawk

Chapter 6: Tommy Orange Tells an Urban Tale   49
Cheyenne and Arapaho

Chapter 7: Rita Joe Finds Her Talk   55
Mi'kmaq

Chapter 8: Marilyn Dumont's Métis Voice   61
Métis

Chapter 9: Jay Odjick Tells a Superhero Story   67
Zibi Anishinabeg

Part 4: Our Stories Bear Witness   73

Chapter 10: Beatriz and Catalina: Court Records Tell Their Story   75
Maya

Chapter 11: Shawnadithit Maps Her Story   83
Beothuk

Chapter 12: Standing Bear: Warrior Witness   89
Oglala Sioux

Woman believed to be Shawnadithit

Chapter 13: Ada Blackjack Kept a Journal   97
Inupiaq

Part 5: Our Hands Tell Our Story   107
Chapter 14: Agnes Yellow Bear Stitches Her Story   109
Plains Cree, Kawactoose First Nation

Chapter 15: Elias Jade Not Afraid Beads His Story   113
Apsaalooke

Chapter 16: The I-Collective Tells the Story with Food   119

Afterword: Our Stories Go On   122
Eldon Yellowhorn, Pikani Nation   124

Sources and Resources   127
Image Credits   130
Index   131

A NOTE ABOUT LANGUAGE AND TERMS

YOU WILL SOMETIMES FIND THE WORDS "Indian" and "Native" in this book, usually when we include a quotation from someone who used those words. Some Indigenous people still use them, but mostly they have fallen out of modern speech.

The word "reservation" is used in the United States. In Canada the word is "reserve." In the United States, reservations usually cover a whole treaty area, while in Canada there can be dozens of reserves within treaty boundaries.

The words used for "schools" in this book may be confusing. In Canada, when Indigenous children were sent far from home, they were sent to "residential schools." Similar schools in the United States were called "boarding schools."

You will see years written in certain ways. When we don't know an exact year, we write c. before the year, like this: "c. 1775" (the *c* stands for *circa,* which means "about" or "approximately"). When we write about someone who is alive today, we give their birth year like this: "b. 1975" (the *b* stands for *born*). For someone who is no longer living, we give the years of their birth and death like this: "1551–1610."

INTRODUCTION: OURS TO TELL

> As native writers, there's a certain feeling that you have to set the record straight before you even begin . . . It's been told wrong, and not told, so often.
>
> —Tommy Orange (Cheyenne and Arapaho), *The New York Times*

THE STORIES PEOPLE TELL ABOUT US MATTER.

Take Thanksgiving. It is a happy time of feasting and family that started when pilgrims shared a friendly meal with Wampanoag people, so the story goes. This is not the story the Wampanoag know.

They recall that in 1621, English colonists invited Chief Massasoit to a feast to mark a land deal. He brought ninety of his men with him. That land deal meal is what is commonly called the first Thanksgiving. Another such meal was held two years later. It was supposed to symbolize eternal friendship. That night, two hundred Wampanoag died. They had been poisoned.

By the time Massasoit's son, Metacomet, became chief, there were no more friendly meals shared. Pilgrims were taking more and more land and forcing their way of life, especially their religion, on the Wampanoag. Metacomet (called King Philip by the English) was forced to sign a peace treaty. Three of his men were hanged, and his brother died mysteriously; some believe he was poisoned by the colonists. This led to King Philip's War, the first full conflict between Indigenous people and white settlers. Fourteen months of fighting followed until Metacomet was killed and his people could fight no more. His head was displayed at the entrance of Plymouth Fort for the next twenty-five years. Those who survived had little reason to give thanks. They were rounded up and sold into slavery.

The Thanksgiving story shows why we tell our own stories. We want our version to be known. We know our own history. In this book you'll meet some of the countless creative Indigenous people who invented symbols, drew maps, painted their history, wrote poems and songs, or kept eyewitness records. There are novelists and craftspeople and cookbook authors and graphic artists here, all with their own story to tell.

Marilyn Dumont

PART 1

We Tell Our Story in Images and Symbols

Our stories come to us from generations of storytellers. To aid the teller's memory, or to capture a thrilling scene, or to leave a record, storytellers have used symbols and images. Indigenous stories have long been recorded in painted pictures on cliffs or animal hides. Sometimes the storyteller scratched figures into birch bark or rock faces.

This section is about two people who used, or invented, images to tell their own stories. A Maya scribe named Gaspar Antonio Chi recorded his story using his people's ancient *glyphs*—symbols—and Sequoyah created new symbols that enabled Cherokee to write on paper.

A petroglyph cave painting in Mexico

A piece of Maya pottery showing a scribe creating Maya art

Chapter 1

GASPAR ANTONIO CHI
Rebel Scribe
Maya, 1531–1610

For at least two thousand years people in Mexico and Central America wrote their stories using glyphs: symbols that stand for words, sounds, or ideas. The Maya carved glyphs into stone monuments and wooden objects, painted them on ceramic dishes, and wrote them on bark paper. The stories they told were mostly about royal families, mighty battles, and their code of laws. When the Spanish invaders arrived, the glyphs—which the Spanish could not read—became a way to keep Maya culture alive.

IMAGINE GASPAR ANTONIO CHI at work. He's a man of noble birth, proud of the title given only to scribes or writers like him: "He of the Holy Book." It gives him the right to wear a special *sarong,* a long piece of cloth, tied around his waist, and a headdress tied around his forehead.

Images of gods and ancestors painted on his workshop's stone walls watch as he burns incense and says a prayer. Then he smooths out a sheet of paper made from the bark of a fig tree and plucks a brush out of the stick bundle tucked into his headdress. Carefully, he dips the brush into precious *sabak,* black ink, that fills an inkpot fashioned from half a conch shell. Only then does he write . . .

Gaspar was a Maya scribe when the Spanish *conquistadors* (conquerors) arrived in Yucatán in the early 1500s. They brought disease and destruction with them. In the Maya text called the *Chilam Balam* the scribe Tizimin wrote:

"How we wept when they came!"

Catholic priests followed the conquistadors to convert the Maya to Christianity. They used their Latin books, painted murals, and plays to teach their beliefs. They used terror to force

Codex Dresdensis, a Maya manuscript from the thirteenth century

A painting by Diego de Landa depicting the destruction of Maya literature

the Maya to give up their own beliefs. They arrested and tortured people who had books about Maya gods or statues or pictures portraying them, as well as anyone suspected of practicing their traditional ways. They burned thousands of books and executed the holders of Traditional Knowledge.

The Maya resisted. They burned down Spanish churches. Many fled to the forests. Others hid their books, sacred objects, and religious practices in caves or remote temples. The Spanish couldn't read Maya glyphs. Scribes realized that their knowledge of how to write using glyphs gave them a secret language and a subtle way to rebel.

Maya glyphic writing consists of *pictographs* that carry meaning, much like logos and icons do today. The Spanish had no idea what the pictographs meant. They relied on local interpreters who could read the glyphic writing.

Although the Spanish bishop Diego de Landa was a relentless book-burner, he was curious about the Maya way of life. Around 1566 he gathered a group of scribes, including Gaspar Chi to help him make a Maya/Spanish alphabet.

Marisol Ceh Moo
Yukatek Maya, b. 1978

You may have read about the mysterious Lost Empire of the Maya. It's an interesting story, but it is wrong. Today, around eight million Maya live throughout Mexico and Central America, roughly as many as when the Spanish invaders first arrived. Some live traditional lives on farms and in small towns. Others have urban lifestyles in cities across North and Central America. Today, they keep their way of life vibrant by teaching their language in schools, producing dictionaries, and encouraging Maya arts.

One keeper of Maya culture is Marisol Ceh Moo from Yucatán, Mexico. She is a Yukatek Maya professor and a writer of novels, short stories, poems, and essays. Her novel *X-Teya, u puksi'ik'al ko'olel* (Teya, Heart of a Woman) is the first written by a woman in the Yukatek language.

He would sound out a letter and Gaspar would draw a Maya symbol for it.

Maya writing is based on syllables, so Gaspar would draw more than one symbol for each word. This made de Landa furious and made Gaspar so frustrated that he wrote a message that he knew de Landa couldn't read: *a in k'ati*, or "I do not wish."

A manuscript page featuring the Maya alphabet

The Landback movement has existed for years to reclaim Indigenous land to the original owners. You could say that Gaspar Chi was an early Landback activist thanks to the book he wrote in glyphs. The "Xiu Family Tree" is a record of every member of the Chi, or *Xiu* family from the fourteenth to sixteenth century and their land rights. Claiming that the Maya land belonged to his family could have gotten him executed. He outwitted the priests by disguising his history as a Christian text. The Spanish never realized that Gaspar had made a legal record so future generations would never forget the story of his family.

The genealogical tree of the Xiu family, created by Gaspar Antonio Chi around 1550–1560

Cherokee artist Traci Rabbit tells a story through a painted scene titled *Land of My Heart*

Chapter 2

SEQUOYAH
Invents a Syllabary
Cherokee, c. 1775–1843

Cherokee always told their stories orally—using spoken words—and in art, but their language didn't have a written form. Sequoyah invented a *syllabary*—a set of symbols where each one stands for a sound that makes up part of a word—so that his Cherokee language could be written down. It gave his people a valuable new tool with which to tell their story.

SEQUOYAH GATHERED FRIENDS, neighbors, and community leaders to explain his invention. Instead of applauding his work, they put him and his six-year-old daughter, A-Yo-Ka, on trial for witchcraft.

One of the men forced a protesting A-Yo-Ka into another room so she couldn't hear. Someone said a few words to Sequoyah. He wrote them down on a slip of paper. A-Yo-Ka was led back in. Sequoyah handed her the paper. She read the message aloud to the astonished gathering. They wondered, *What kind of power did that paper have?*

Sequoyah was born around 1775 in Taskigi, North Carolina. His Cherokee mother, Wuh-teh, of the Paint Clan, raised him. He worked among white settlers, learning to be a blacksmith and then a silversmith. He saw his white neighbors writing their thoughts on paper to make what the Cherokee called "talking leaves." When he served in the Cherokee Regiment during the War of 1812, he saw how useful writing was to send messages to other units or to write letters home. He thought his people could do that too.

Sequoyah was nearly forty years old when he began working on a Cherokee syllabary. For the next twelve years he was obsessed with ways to capture the Cherokee language in pen and ink.

The Cherokee alphabet prepared by Sequoyah

Everybody laughed at him for wasting his time. Even his own relatives begged him to give it up and focus on taking care of his family. He didn't listen.

Sequoyah first tried drawing a different symbol for every single word in his language. Soon he realized that this would be a huge task for him, and for anybody who had to memorize thousands of symbols. Instead, he listened carefully to Cherokee speech, breaking each word apart into its basic sounds. Then he assigned a symbol to each sound. He invented eighty-six symbols representing *syllables*: the parts of words made up of combinations of consonant and vowel sounds. Cherokee would be the very first Indigenous language written in syllabic form.

Soon suspicion gave way to enthusiasm for Sequoyah's syllabary. In 1821 the Cherokee Council adopted it, and for the first time they could read and write in their own language. Within six months at least 25 percent of Cherokee could use the syllabary. Three years later, three times as many Cherokee could read their language than their white neighbors could read English.

Sequoyah relocated his family to Oklahoma in 1832 to avoid white violence. In 1839 he helped Cherokee flee from Texas, where they were often in danger from settlers. Two years later, he set out to find a lost band of Cherokee he believed had wandered far south. He planned to teach them his syllabary and to reunite them with the rest of the Cherokee Nation. He went as far as Mexico, but he never came back. He died in August 1843.

The Cherokee Nation is now located in Oklahoma, where Cherokee and English are the official languages. Sequoyah's syllabary is still in use. It is taught in schools and symbols appear on street signs and buildings around the community.

Sequoyah gave his people a new way to tell their story. All the while, he stayed faithful to his traditions. He never adopted white clothing, religion, or other customs. The only language people ever heard him speak was Cherokee. Historians debate whether he learned to read or write in English.

Street signs in Cherokee and English on the Cherokee Indian Reservation in North Carolina

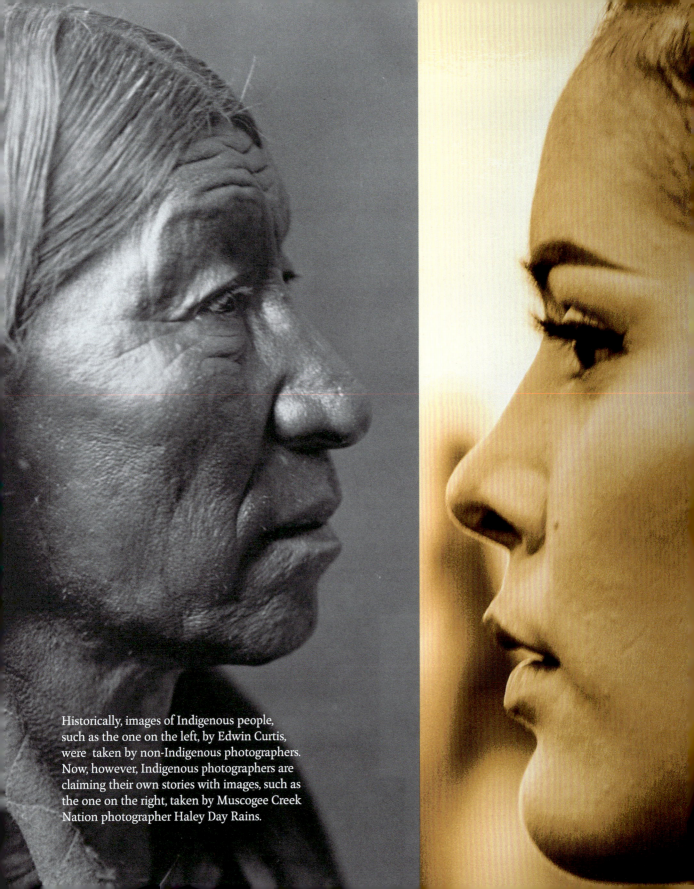

Historically, images of Indigenous people, such as the one on the left, by Edwin Curtis, were taken by non-Indigenous photographers. Now, however, Indigenous photographers are claiming their own stories with images, such as the one on the right, taken by Muscogee Creek Nation photographer Haley Day Rains.

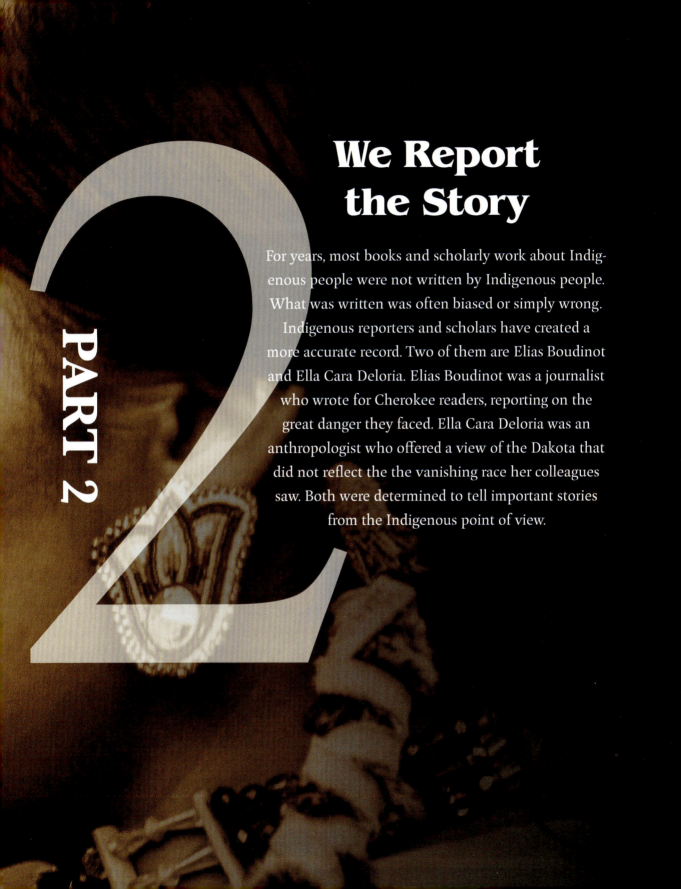

PART 2

We Report the Story

For years, most books and scholarly work about Indigenous people were not written by Indigenous people. What was written was often biased or simply wrong. Indigenous reporters and scholars have created a more accurate record. Two of them are Elias Boudinot and Ella Cara Deloria. Elias Boudinot was a journalist who wrote for Cherokee readers, reporting on the great danger they faced. Ella Cara Deloria was an anthropologist who offered a view of the Dakota that did not reflect the the vanishing race her colleagues saw. Both were determined to tell important stories from the Indigenous point of view.

ᏣᎳᎩ ᏣᎳᎩ ᎠᎢᏍᏗ

CHEROKEE PHOENIX

NEW ECHOTA, THURSDAY FEBRUARY 21, 18[28]

...UDINOTT.
BY
...RRIS,
...TION.
...ce, $3 in six
he end of the

read only the
will be $2,00
aid within the

considered as
give notice to
...encement of a

...d on a Super-
ly new procur-
...son procuring
ng responsible
...ive a seventh

...erted at seven-
... the first in-
half cents for
...nes in propor-

to the Editor,
...tention.

S Ꭹ Ꭱ Ꮿ Ꭷ Ꭲ
...ᏙᎯ ᏋᎴᏗ
ᎠᎠ ᏋᎳᏗ
ᎠᎴᎭᎨᎢ, ᏐᎢ
...ᏋᎵ ᎴᎠᏗ, ᏋᎢ
... ᏚᎢᎪ ᏘᎴ ᏊᎢ
...ᎴᏓᎬᏁ ᏚᎾ
...ᎤᎨᎠᎢ ᎦᎭᏕ ᎠᏛᎠᎨᎢ-
... Ꮽ ᏓᏐ ᎠᎹ
Ꮓ ᎢᏚᏣᏐ ᎠᎵ
Ꮾ ᏦᎠᎡᏓ

CONSTITUTION OF THE CHE-
ROKEE NATION,

Formed by a Convention of Delegates from the several Districts, at New Echota, July 1827.

WE, THE REPRESENTATIVES of the people of the CHEROKEE NATION in Convention assembled, in order to establish justice, ensure tranquility, promote our common welfare, and secure to ourselves and our posterity the blessings of liberty; acknowledging with humility and gratitude the goodness of the sovereign Ruler of the Universe, in offering us an opportunity so favorable to the design, and imploring his aid and direction in its accomplishment, do ordain and establish this Constitution for the Government of the Cherokee Nation.

ARTICLE I.

SEC. 1. THE BOUNDARIES of this nation, embracing the lands solemnly guaranteed and reserved forever to the Cherokee Nation by the Treaties concluded with the United States, are as follows; and shall forever hereafter remain unalterably the same—to wit: Beginning on the North Bank of Tennessee River at the upper part of the Chickasaw old fields; thence along the main channel of said river, including all the islands therein, to the mouth of the Hiwassee river, thence up the main channel of said river, including Islands, to the first hill which

First issue of the Cherokee Phoenix, February 21, 1828

ᎫᏲᏣᎴᎠᎢ ᏣᎳᎩ ᎤᎾᏚᏏ.

ᏣᎠᏫ ᏔᏌᎩ ᎮᎢᏁᎦᎦ ᎤᏍᎶᎠ, ᏓᏛᎯ ᎤᎠᏛ ᎤᎯᎠᎨᎦ.

ᎠᏢ ᎡᎭᏢ ᎠᎦᎭᎵᏢ ᎠᏌᎢ ᎵᎠᏍᏫ, ᏣᎳᎩ ᎤᎤᏍᎡ ᎠᎩᏞᎨᎦ, ᏍᎦᎠᏢ ᏗᎩᎯᎶᎠᎴ, ᎠᏊ ᎠᎠ ᏣᎩᎤᎦᎣᎴᎴ, ᎠᏊ ᎠᏥ ᏔᎡᏢᎡᎵᎭ ᏆᏂᏃ ᏃᏓ ᎩᎳᎩ ᎠᏌᎢ ᏋᏳᏕᏋᏘᎴᎢ, ᎣᎭᏤ ᏕᎢᎭᏞᎠᎴᎢ ᎦᏕᎪ ᎩᏋᎴᏘ ᎸᏢᎡᎣ ᏍᎩ, ᎠᏊ ᏞᏢᎭ ᎣᎭᏤ ᎣᎠᎩ ᏔᏠᎢ ᎸᎴᏋᎴᎦᎣ, ᏋᏳᏉᎢᎠ, ᎠᏛ ᎫᏲᏣᎴᎠᎢ ᎩᎳᎩ ᎤᎤᏝᏋ ᎤᎴᎰ. ᏍᎠᎳᎵᏉ ᎡᎠ, ᏞᎡᏊᏢ ᎣᎡᏳᎦᎠ, ᏀᏞᎠᏣᎩ; ᎠᏊ ᎠᎦᎨᎴᎸᎳ ᎣᎭᏤ ᏔᏤᎳᎢᏛᏢ ᏍᎩ ᎠᏛ ᎣᎭᏤ ᏔᏠᎢ ᏋᏳᏉᎢᎠ ᏳᏥᏢᎴᎵᎰᎭ, ᎠᏊ ᎣᎭᏤ ᏓᏛᎲᎠᎵᎠ, ᎠᏊ ᏍᎴᎳᎴ, ᏀᎳᎸᎰ.

I.

1. ᎠᎦᎪᏢ ᏞᎦᏞᎵ ᎠᏛᎩᎳᎩ ᎤᎤᏝᏆ ᎦᎠᏞ, ᎣᎭᎴᎪᎦᎠ ᎵᎡᏢᏂᎡᎦᏞ ᏍᎦᎠᏢ, ᎠᏊ ᎡᏥᎭᎠ ᎧᎦᎡᎦ ᏍᎩ, ᎣᏋᏢᎰ ᏒᎤᎨᎰᎩᎦᎣ, ᎠᏛ ᎦᎠᎢ; ᎠᏊ ᎣᎭᏤᏳᎠ ᎦᎳᏎᎳ ᏓᎠᎠ ᎣᎳᎦᎨᎠᎵ ᎸᏢᎡᎣ ᏆᏂᏃ. ᎸᏍᎢ ᎣᎭᏒᏍᎤᏔ ᏫᏋᎦ ᎣᎳᏋᏔ ᏔᎴᏍᎪᎳᎠᎴᎵᎪᎦᎣ, ᎣᎭᏤ ᎣᎢᎦ ᎡᎴᎦᎠᎢ, ᎭᏍᏔ ᎠᏗᎦᎦ ᏎᏌᎤᎴ ᎩᎳᎩ ᏌᎧᎠᏍ, ᎠᏊᎬᎳ ᎣᏆᎬ ᎣᎳᏋ ᏓᎠᎴᎦᎦ ᎠᏊᎬᎳ ᎣᏍᎾᎭᏔᎠᎴᎢ, ᏖᏢ ᏔᎦᏨᎰᎰ ᎧᎩ ᎠᎬᎳᏋ ᎠᎦᎾᎰᏔ, ᎠᎦᏢ ᎠᏊ ᏎᎠᏔ ᎣᎭᏤᎳᏢ ᎩᎳᎩ ᏌᎧᎠᏍ. ᎣᎤᎠᏋ ᎣᎤᏔᏞᎥᏛ, ᎠᏊᎬᎳ ᎴᎴᎦ ᏎᎠᏋ ᎸᏍᎦᎦᎣᏔ, ᏓᎠᎴᎦᎦ, ᏗᏁᎭ ᎰᎠᏋ ᎣᎤᏋ ᏣᎴᎴᎵᏞᎠᎴᏔ. ᎣᎳᏛ ᏓᏊ ᎣᎭᏤᏳᎠ ᏔᎴᎳᏋᎭᏆ, ᏓᎠᏛ ᎣᎴᏛᎫᎠ ᏛᏢᏞᏔ ᎠᎣᎦᎢ; ᏗᏁᎭ ᎠᏊ ᎩᎳᎩ ᏌᎧᎠᏍ. ᎣᎤᎠᏋᏃ ᎣᎣᎴᏞᎴᎢ, ᎠᏊᎬᎳ ᎵᎡᏨ ᏌᏋ ᎭᏍᎨᎪᎠᎩ ᎠᏔᎦᏍᏍ, ᏝᎶ ᏋᏋ ᎣᎤᏋ ᎭᎴᎵᏔᎠᎴᎵ ᎣᎤᎠᏋ ᏐᎦᎠ ᏓᎠᎳᏢᎬᎳ ᏣᎧᎡᎠ ᎤᎳᎬᏔ ᎤᎳᎡᏢ ᎣᎠ

readmission. Moreover... ture shall have powe[r] laws and regulations may deem expedient prevent the citizens ing improvements wi[th] speculation.

ARTICLE [II.]
SEC. 1. THE Pow[er of the Go-] vernment shall be di[vided into three] distinct departments [: the Legisla-] tive, the Executive, [and the Judicial.]
SEC. 2. No perso[n or persons be-] longing to one of thes[e departments] shall exercise any of [the powers pro-] perly belonging to e[ither of the oth-] ers, except in the c[ases hereafter] expressly directed o[r permitted.]

ARTICL[E III.]
SEC. 1. THE LEG[ISLATIVE POWER] shall be vested [in two distinct] branches; a Comm[ittee and a Coun-] cil; each to have a [negative on the] other, and both to be [styled, The Gene-] ral Council of the C[herokee Nation;] and the style of thei[r acts and laws] shall be,
"Resolved by th[e Committee and] Council in General [Council convene-] ed."
SEC. 2. The Che[rokee Nation shall be] laid off into eight D[istricts, which shall] remain.
SEC. 3. The Co[mmittee shall con-] sist of two member[s from each Dis-] trict, and the Counc[il shall consist of] three members from

Chapter 3

ELIAS BOUDINOT'S
Story Was a Warning
Cherokee, 1804–1839

When Sequoyah created his syllabary, Cherokee were eager to learn how to make their own "talking leaves"—writing on paper. In 1825 the Cherokee National Council, at their capital in New Echota, Georgia, officially accepted Sequoyah's syllabary. They used it to write the laws of their nation and to launch their own newspaper, the *Cherokee Phoenix*, using a special new typeface. Elias Boudinot was one of the first Indigenous journalists who used it to warn his Cherokee readers about the calamity that was unfolding.

BORN IN 1804, ELIAS WAS A young boy when war broke out between the Americans and the British in 1812. Cherokee warriors chose to fight alongside the Americans. Despite their allegiance, they got nothing when the war ended in 1814. Georgia state officials and citizens began a campaign of harassment, intimidation, and murder against them. Their goal was to remove the entire Cherokee nation from its homeland to the "Indian Country" west of the Mississippi River.

Elias's parents, Oo-watie and Susanna Reese, had named their son Gallegina, but his family and friends all called him Buck Watie. As a young man, he concluded that the only chance for the Cherokee to survive as a people was to learn the ways of settlers, including their ways of education. His local school offered only the basics. If he wanted more settler education, he would have to leave home.

Buck Watie was thirteen years old when he set out with a group of students to attend the Foreign Mission School in Connecticut. A man named Elias Boudinot, the president of the American Bible Society, hosted the students on their travels. Buck Watie respected the old man so much that he decided to rename himself. When he arrived at the Foreign Mission School he registered as Elias Boudinot and never used his childhood name again.

Elias was a young student when he became one of the first people to learn Sequoyah's syllabary. When he returned home in 1822, he and a missionary, Samuel Worcester, used the syllabary to translate the New Testament into Cherokee and produced a hymn book.

Newspapers in Georgia regularly printed biased stories against Cherokee.

Cherokee printing press in Gordon County, Georgia

The Cherokee Council decided the best way to counter the propaganda was to have a community-owned newspaper that printed accurate news. But starting a newspaper did not happen overnight, especially when the people involved had no tradition of writing. They had to create everything from nothing. They had to buy a printing press, and they needed lead type both for English letters and for the Cherokee syllabary.

Elias took charge of raising funds for the newspaper. Two years later the Council launched an office in New Echota, hiring Elias to be the editor.

A missionary society had the metal type for the Cherokee syllabary cast in Boston. The type, the printing press, and furniture were delivered by steamship to Augusta, Georgia, late in 1827, and then hauled by wagon to the newspaper office in New Echota, over 322 kilometers (two hundred miles) inland. The load weighed well over a tonne and the traveling conditions were difficult, so progress was slow. Finally, in early 1828 the Cherokee took delivery of the press. After assembling it, Elias published the first edition of the *Cherokee Phoenix* on February 21, 1828.

For the next six years the *Cherokee Phoenix* was the voice of the Cherokee Nation at a time when the politics of the day threatened its existence. Pressure from the federal government had already forced

Cast metal type in the Cherokee syllabary

many Cherokee from their homelands, splitting their nation between east and west. The newspaper kept them informed and united about the government's planned land grab.

The paper reported on Sequoyah's trip to Washington as part of a delegation to argue against the proposed Indian Removal Act. Under the act, more than forty-six thousand Indigenous people would be forced to leave their twenty-five million acres of fertile land and forests to "resettle" in "Indian Territory," which is now known as Oklahoma. The delegation's efforts failed, and in 1830, the United States Congress passed the Indian Removal Act. Pressure began to mount on the Cherokee to leave their country. When prospectors discovered gold on their land, the cries for removal grew even louder.

From his travels around Georgia and the United States, Elias grew to believe that uprooting the nation from its ancient land was inevitable. His people had become a minority in their own country. He knew that the Americans were intent on taking the land for themselves, even if that meant exterminating all Cherokee. He was certain there would be no room for the Cherokee Nation in the new republic.

He wanted to publish his opinion in the newspaper, but fellow Cherokee who opposed removal wouldn't let him. In the summer of 1832, he resigned over the dispute.

Elijah Hicks then served as editor until the *Cherokee Phoenix* published its final edition on May 31, 1834. After that, the Cherokee Council ran out of money for their newspaper. They lost the only voice they had to argue against removal from their ancient homeland. Their print shop grew quiet, and the press sat idle for nearly a year. When state officials discovered the plan to start printing the newspaper again in 1835, they sent in the Georgia Guard to confiscate the press. They took it apart and threw away the pieces.

In the Treaty of New Echota of December 1835, the Cherokee received $5 million and a reservation in Indian Territory (Oklahoma) in exchange for their seven million acres of ancestral land. Most Cherokee opposed the treaty. Elias Boudinot was one of the people who signed it. The signers thought that if they couldn't stop the removal, they might at least be able to get better terms for their people.

In October 1838, eight years after the Indian Removal Act was passed, the Cherokee were rounded up and banished to the Indian Territory west of the Mississippi River. They were defenseless against the white mobs that burned their crops, their orchards, and their farms. Over six months, as they made the forced march to Oklahoma, more than four thousand people died of starvation, exposure to extreme weather, and disease along what they called the Trail of Tears.

Like Sequoyah, Elias did not walk the Trail of Tears. He had left with his family in 1837 to a make a new home in the west, thinking that someone had to be there to receive the rest of his people when they arrived. He didn't know that many of his Cherokee kin thought he was a traitor and blamed him for their suffering. He was only thirty-five years old when an assailant killed him for signing the Treaty of New Echota.

Although he left a troubled legacy, Elias Boudinot was the founder of Indigenous journalism in North America.

Indigenous journalism and the idea of community newspapers went quiet until the twentieth century, when Indigenous people across North America finally had the resources start the presses again. Even the *Cherokee Phoenix* rose once more and is today bringing news to the Cherokee Nation. Unlike the original journal, it publishes in English only. However, it appears in print and in a digital format on the Internet. It is a popular national newspaper.

> Today the *Cherokee Phoenix* reports on the tribe's government, current events, and Cherokee culture, people, and history, broadening its outreach to include locally aired radio shows, Facebook posts, X feeds, Instagram profiles, and a YouTube channel.

Members of the Standing Rock Sioux Tribe of North and South Dakota in the 1940s

Chapter 4

ELLA CARA DELORIA'S
Insider Story
Yankton Sioux, 1889–1971

Indigenous people have been studied by many outsiders, mostly European *anthropologists*—scientists who study the norms and values of human cultures. Ella Cara Deloria was different. She was an anthropologist too, but she was no outsider. The people she studied were her own.

I try to keep out of it, but I am too much in it, and I know too many angles. If the outside investigator is like a naturalist watching ants, and reporting what he sees, and draws conclusions from that, I am one of the ants! I know what the fight is about, what all the other little ants are saying under their breath! I did think it would be such a cinch!

—Ella Cara Deloria,
February 13, 1947,
letter to Ruth Benedict

ELLA CARA DELORIA WAS BORN to the Yankton Sioux on January 31, 1889. Despite the blizzard that raged outside, her parents gave her a hopeful name: Anpetu Waste-win, or Beautiful Day Woman.

Ella's father, Black Lodge (Tipi Sapa), was a Yankton chief and one of the first Sioux to become an Episcopal priest. In 1890, Black Lodge was put in charge of St. Elizabeth's church and the boarding school at Wakpala, South Dakota, on Standing Rock Reservation. Many of the people there were Hunkpapa and Blackfoot Teton (Lakota). Ella grew up speaking two Sioux dialects and knowing about both the Episcopal religion and traditional Sioux beliefs.

Ella won a scholarship to Oberlin College in 1910 and went on to get a degree at Columbia Teachers College. That's where she met Franz Boas, who was a professor at Columbia University. He was one of the founders of modern anthropology. When he began his career, anthropologists thought that all

Frank Boas, one of the founders of modern anthropology, recruited Ella Cara Deloria to study her people.

societies developed through what were called savage and barbaric stages until they reached what resembled European civilization. Boas had a radical idea: He proposed that though cultures were different, they couldn't be ranked on such a scale. They had to be understood in the context of their history, where they were located, and what they believed. This was a bombshell of an idea for white Europeans, who assumed that their way of life was the best there was. Ella's work would help show that Indigenous societies were as complex and vibrant as any others. They weren't the vanishing race so many assumed. They were adapting.

Boas had Ella check what *linguists* (people who study languages) and travelers on the Plains had already written about the Lakota. One of those people was a doctor named James R. Walker. He wrote detailed notes describing religious practices, and he measured the skulls of Lakota men, women, and children. (Anthropologists at the time were obsessed with measuring people, especially their skulls. They assumed the bigger your skull, the bigger your brain,

A family stands in front of their home in Standing Rock.

Vine Deloria Jr.
Standing Rock Sioux, 1933–2005

Vine Deloria Jr., Ella's nephew, was a prominent writer, thinker, and activist in the fight for the rights of Native Americans. His 1969 book, *Custer Died for Your Sins: An Indian Manifesto*, challenged the standard historical narrative of America by highlighting the oppression of Indigenous people. He was a sharp critic of anthropologists, in part because of the poor treatment his aunt received.

and therefore the smarter you are. This is false, but it reinforced ideas that one race could be superior to another.)

When Ella got to Pine Ridge, South Dakota, she found that James had misunderstood what he heard. Since he didn't speak any of the Sioux dialects, he didn't realize that the Lakota had told him the way things were supposed to be, or the way things used to be, not the way things were in the present. He often interviewed the wrong people. Ella, who knew the role each person had in the community, wrote, "I have seen white people questioning someone who is regarded as a fool in the tribe, and quoting him as gospel, and I have seen the real people of the tribe laughing at him."

Ella had a great advantage. "I stand on middle ground and know both sides," she wrote.

She knew that it was proper to take a gift of food when she visited someone she was interviewing. She knew how to eat properly when she was a guest. She knew the right terms to use when she talked to someone. There are many ways to say uncle, brother, sister, aunt, or cousin in Sioux languages. In these ways, the Lakota knew she was one of them, not an outside observer.

Despite her skills as an anthropologist, Ella faced big challenges. Writing never came easily to her. In a letter to famous anthropologist Ruth Benedict, she complained of writer's block: "Ruth, it's just awful! I simply cannot write. . . . There is too much I know. I made a hundred false starts and can't tell you how many times I've torn up my [manuscript] and begun again." Another problem was money. Despite all her valuable work, Ella was paid poorly. She once said that she owned only six things, none of which was a typewriter. During the 1940s, when she was in her mid-fifties, Ella could seldom pay her rent on time. Some frigid South Dakota winters, she could afford to heat only one room. She sometimes lived in her ancient car.

Despite the challenges with writer's block and poverty, she kept working on three manuscripts. One was *Speaking of Indians*. It corrected the mistaken impressions of missionaries while defending traditional Lakota culture, especially religion. *The Dakota Way of Life* is an *ethnography* (a scientific description of a culture) for anthropologists. Her novel *Waterlily* was about three generations of women before the time of reservations. It was written for people who like a good romance. *Waterlily* explores the religious life, hopes, and dreams of Lakota women, set against fascinating details of daily life. For instance, she describes girls bowling on the ice with round stones while old women stay warm inside a tepee playing a plum-pit game, which is much like shooting dice.

She finished *Waterlily* in 1948, but nobody would publish it. Ella had a series of strokes in 1970 and died the following year while working on a Lakota dictionary. In 1988, seventeen years after her death, *Waterlily* finally appeared in print. Now it is praised as an important work in feminist literature.

Ella's writing shows us a people who could adapt, a language that's incredibly expressive, and the lives of women who are often overlooked. These are stories only an insider could tell.

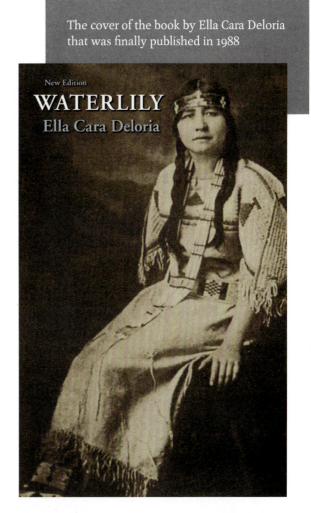

The cover of the book by Ella Cara Deloria that was finally published in 1988

Tim Fontaine Tells the Story with Satire

Sagkeeng First Nation, Manitoba

Walking Eagle News is a satirical digital newspaper established in 2017. It jokingly calls itself "the foremost leader in the world of Indigenous journalism." The stories are made up, but, incredibly, they are always based on real events.

When some school boards in Canada worried about teaching too much Indigenous curriculum, this was the headline in *Walking Eagle News*:

"Parents Upset after Indigenous Curriculum Turns Kids into First Nation, Métis, Inuit Peoples."

The satirical article reads: "'I'm all for having our children learn about this country's history but could my daughter at least have been changed into a girl her own age?' said Melissa Mitchell, a Regina mother whose 11-year-old daughter Liz returned home as an 87-year-old Inuk Elder."

When police were supposed to investigate a man who drove a truck through a crowd of Indigenous people on a memorial march for residential school survivors, *Walking Eagle News* reported: "RCMP say investigators playing 'fun game of hide and seek' with people who witnessed man drive truck into crowd of Indigenous people."

When *Walking Eagle News* ran the headline "Indigenous People, Stop Eating Our Animals So We Can Kill Them for Sport: Hunting Organization," readers were reminded of violent clashes over who has the right to hunt and fish—people who do it only for sport, or Indigenous people who hunt to have food to eat.

Tim Fontaine is the brilliant mind behind *Walking Eagle News*. For twenty years he was what he calls a "serious journalist." He says he founded *Walking Eagle News* as a way of "setting his illustrious journalism career on fire and dancing in its ashes."

One day in 2017 he stood up after a meeting, announced that he was quitting his job as a journalist, and walked out of the building, thinking that this was the end of his career.

He launched *Walking Eagle News* because it would let him combine his interest in the news with his love of humor, and because he thought it would be fun.

Tim isn't out to mislead people or make a fool out of anyone. His humor is aimed at the way that Indigenous news is reported in the mainstream press.

Funny as it is, everything on *Walking Eagle News* has a serious purpose. Tim says: "*Walking Eagle* is me telling the world, 'This is what it feels like.'"

Ella Cara Deloria wears the traditional clothing of the Sioux in 1930

Ella Cara Deloria's book was not published for seventeen years after she wrote it.

From left to right: Tommy Orange, Rita Joe, and Marilyn Dumont

PART 3

Our History Is in Our Poems, Songs, and Written Stories

From the beginning, we have told origin stories about how the world was created, stories about the deeds of gods and heroes, and stories that teach us lessons. Our stories are funny or sad or full of action—and often all three—so that we will remember the characters and the lessons in each one.

In Blackfoot tradition, the tales were so entertaining that they distracted people from their work. There was a taboo against sharing stories during the summer, the season when people were supposed to be working hard to get ready for winter.

The people you will meet here are only a few of the thousands of poets, songwriters, novelists, and cartoonists who have built on that Oral Tradition. They are telling the Indigenous story to readers in powerful and inventive ways.

A promotional bill for Pauline Johnson's American Chautauqua Tour in 1907

Chapter 5

PAULINE JOHNSON
Poet Pop Star
Mohawk, 1861–1913

Poet Pauline Johnson was a star. She criss-crossed North America nineteen times, reading her poetry to captivated audiences in big cities and the small towns that had grown along the new rail routes. Her mother had read her English ballads and poetry. She adapted their style to the woodlands and lakes she loved. But her poems also embraced her Haudenosaunee heritage.

AS A YOUNG GIRL GROWING UP by the Grand River in Ontario, Pauline Johnson would launch her canoe into the water and float in quiet solitude. Inspired by the rhythm of her paddle, she composed her poems. For Pauline, canoeing was a passion and a pastime she never abandoned, even after she became one of the pop stars of her time.

Pauline was born in 1861 on the Six Nations reserve near Brantford, Ontario. (Her full name was Emily Pauline Johnson and she is sometimes referred to as E. Pauline Johnson.) She was the youngest in the family of Onwanonsyshon, the Mohawk chief known as George Johnson, and his English bride Emily Howells.

Her father died when she was twenty-three. Her mother moved the family from the reserve, the only home Pauline had known, to Brantford, Ontario. A well-raised young lady like Pauline should have been learning how to manage a household so she'd be a good wife. Pauline had other ideas. She wrote poetry.

At that time, all entertainment was live. Long before radio or television, people flocked to lectures and poetry readings to be amused, astonished, or moved to tears. Pauline started reciting her own poetry in public and discovered that she had a flair for performing.

Taking the stage name Tekahionwake, meaning "Double Wampum," she made

Pauline Johnson canoeing

up characters who acted out her poetry. The Mohawk Woman and the English Lady were her favorite roles. Act 1 of her performance began with her stepping in front of the stage lights with flowing hair, wearing a buckskin dress, a bear-claw necklace, and a wampum belt. At the intermission she pulled her hair into a bun, put on a fashionable gown and frilly hat, swapped her comfortable moccasins for dainty heeled slippers, and returned for Act 2. Audiences loved it.

In the winter of 1892 Pauline was invited to recite a poem for an audience in Toronto. She glided into the spotlight wearing a pale gray silk gown. She stood in the center of the stage silently until not a sound was heard in the room. Then, projecting her lovely voice, she began to recite from "A Cry from an Indian Wife." She included it in her 1912 book *Flint and Feather*:

The performer Pauline Johnson in her Indigenous regalia

Go forth, nor bend to greed of white men's hands,

By right, by birth we Indians own these lands,

Though starved, crushed, plundered, lies our nation low . . .

Perhaps the white man's God has willed it so.

She enjoyed the thunderous applause she heard. Invitations to tour poured in.

Her one-woman show enthralled audiences in the eastern parts of Canada and the United States. She rode the transcontinental train from Ontario to Vancouver, British Columbia, stopping in cities and towns along the route to perform her poems. Despite her fame, her sold-out performances earned her only enough money to support herself and her family.

Her fans couldn't get enough of her. In 1895 she traveled to London, England, for the first time to perform for thrilled Londoners. While she was there, she collected her published poems into a book that she titled *The White Wampum*.

Despite her great success in London, Pauline returned to a life of poverty in Canada. When her mother died in 1898, Pauline was an adult at thirty-seven years old, but she felt like an orphan. She had always been single but now she was truly alone. No matter where she traveled, her mother's presence had always drawn her back to Brantford. Now she was like a boat without an anchor.

All her fame didn't protect her from frequent taunts hurled at her. She challenged society's ideas of what a lady was supposed to be like. In her day, women were married by the time they were twenty. As a single woman approaching forty, she became the target of sexist shaming. Racist hecklers called her names because she was Indigenous. Despite all the hardships she faced, Pauline gathered her strength and decided to forge a new life for herself.

The stage helped to soothe the sting of verbal abuse, discrimination, insults, and harassment directed at her. Poetry was her way to fight back at the racism and sexism that filled her life.

In 1905 she was about to retire when she received another invitation to perform in London. She reached Halifax by train and booked passage on a steam ship in the late spring of 1906.

In London she became one of the stars

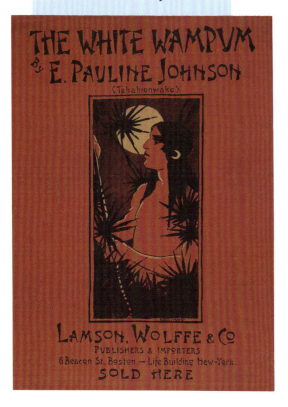

The cover of the book *The White Wampum*, a collection of Pauline Johnson's poems

of the summer theater circuit. She settled into a routine of visiting sights in the city between performances. One day in August she met a Squamish leader, Joe Capilano. He was part of a group of Indigenous people from the West Coast of Canada who were in England to meet with King Edward VII. She and Joe became friends and spent much of their free time together. As summer waned, they both prepared to sail back to Canada. Before she left, Joe invited her to visit him on the West Coast. Pauline was forty-five years old in 1906, and the years of travel and performing had taken the gleam off show business for her.

When she returned home, she was diagnosed with breast cancer. She had no time to waste. She decided to take a new path: she would move to the West Coast

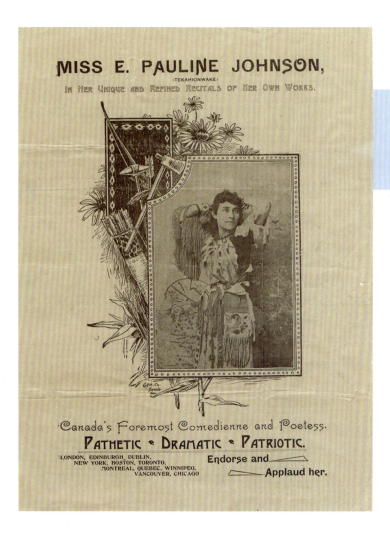

A poster promoting Pauline Johnson's tour in Great Britain and North America

and write prose. In the spring of 1907 when the ice melted off the Grand River, she made a final trip to the water's edge. She found her old canoe and launched it into the lazy current one last time. After a few hours of paddling, she landed her vessel and left it by the riverbank. The next day she boarded the train that would take her to Vancouver, British Columbia.

Her trip took her through several cities across the Prairies where she put on live shows for eager audiences. Newspapers in towns along the railway printed stories and reviews about her visit. News of her arrival reached the city of Vancouver before she did, so a large crowd gathered at the train station to welcome her.

Among them was Joe. The two instantly renewed their friendship and he introduced her to his wife, Mary. Once she settled into an apartment, the three of them often walked to the edge of the city where the trails into Stanley Park begin. Sometimes they would paddle canoes along the shoreline to visit sites that were important to the Squamish. Joe and Mary taught her to observe the tide ebbing and flowing and to recognize the slack tide, which meant calm waters for easy paddling to cross the Burrard Inlet.

Joe and Mary took pleasure in sharing their traditional stories. Each time they reached a landmark, the time was right for another story. Pauline wrote them down, adding her own flourishes, and the newspaper published them.

Pauline and Joe shared more than stories. They were both in poor health. She told him about her cancer, and he told her about his tuberculosis. While she was celebrating her forty-ninth birthday, on March 10, 1910, her friend Joe died.

Chief Joe Capilano, also known as Chief Mathias Joe, was a close friend of Pauline Johnson.

The stories Joe and Mary had shared with Pauline were compiled into one book, called *Legends of Vancouver*. It is still in print and is a popular book of Squamish stories.

Pauline Johnson compiled traditional stories she heard from Joe and Mary Capilano into a collection titled *Legends of Vancouver*.

Pauline lived for two more years, with ever-worsening health. She died on March 7, 1913. Businesses and stores across the city of Vancouver closed that day in her honor. The day of her funeral was also the anniversary of her birth. She would have been fifty-two years old. There is a monument to her in the city's famous Stanley Park. It is where her ashes remain.

Pauline didn't tell the story society expected of her. Instead, she told her own story. She didn't marry, she supported herself and her family, and she blended her two heritages in poems that still have the power to move us.

A memorial honoring Pauline Johnson stands in Stanley Park, Vancouver.

Young dancers participate in the Julyamsh powwow in 2016 in Coeur d'Alene, Idaho.

Chapter 6

TOMMY ORANGE
Tells an Urban Tale
Cheyenne and Arapaho, b. 1982

Indigenous people and their lifeways in the past or on reservations or the land fill the pages of many books. Tommy Orange is from a big city—Oakland, California. He didn't know of any books that showed the way of life he and his friends knew, so he set out to write one.

Urban Indians feel at home walking in the shadow of a downtown building. We came to know the downtown Oakland skyline better than we did any sacred mountain range, the redwoods in the Oakland hills better than any other deep wild forest. We know the sound of the freeway better than we do rivers, the howl of distant trains better than wolf howls. We know the smell of gas and freshly wet concrete and burned rubber better than we do the smell of cedar or sage or even frybread . . . We ride buses, trains and cars over and under concrete plains. Being Indian has never been about returning to the land. The land is everywhere or nowhere.

—Tommy Orange, *There There*

TOMMY ORANGE GREW UP straddling two worlds. He was raised by a Cheyenne father who was an Elder in the Native American Church, and a mother who was a white hippie. She became an evangelical Christian, calling his father's religion the work of the devil. Homelife was confusing. Tommy didn't know what to believe. He worried that the world was about to end and that he might go to hell. His parents eventually divorced.

He also had to figure out where he belonged at school. When he and his father would go to Oklahoma to visit his father's reservation, Tommy always felt clear about his Cheyenne identity. But back in Oakland his mixed-race heritage only inspired confusion. To make matters worse, he went to a high school where most of the kids were white. They often called him racial slurs, but even the taunts didn't fit him. The kids thought he was Latino or Asian. He grew angry that they couldn't even make fun of him properly.

Tommy didn't like school. He wasn't a good student, and he wasn't interested in reading. Instead, he threw himself into roller hockey, and then music when he got a guitar for his eighteenth birthday. After high school he went to college to study audio engineering, hoping to compose piano scores for movies.

There weren't many jobs for composers, so he took whatever job came his way. He was working at a used bookshop when, for something to do, he started reading the books. Fiction was new to him. He quickly fell in love with novels.

A lot of books he read about Indigenous people were about reservation life or living close to the land. He knew this wasn't the reality for everyone. Seventy percent of Indigenous people live in cities, yet it was as if he and his friends were invisible.

The idea for his book *There There* came to him in 2010. He and his wife were driving to a piano concert when he decided he'd write a sort of field guide to city life for Indigenous people.

He drew on some of his own experiences as he started to map out *There There.* He had worked on a storytelling project, listening to people tell their own stories, and he realized he would need at least twelve characters to show how many ways there are to be Indigenous in Oakland. He had also worked on powwow committees helping to plan huge gatherings of singers and drummers in spectacular regalia that brought many tribes together. A powwow would be a perfect setting for his characters lives to come together too.

There There isn't a traditional book. It is fiction but its prologue is non-fiction, leading with a disturbing description of Indigenous men's heads as symbols: on nickels, on sports uniforms, and even on the test-pattern head in a headdress that appeared on screens in the early days of television. Tommy doesn't spare the reader. He wants to remind us of the times when Indigenous people were massacred and their heads were displayed on pikes, just like the Wampanoag Chief Metacomet. He does a deep dive into the traumas his characters and their ancestors endured. He starts his present-day novel

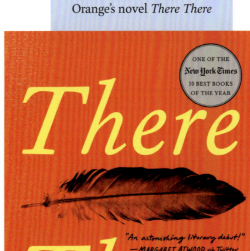

The cover of Tommy Orange's novel *There There*

Urban Indigeneity

Children attend an after-school program at the Little Earth of United Tribes housing complex in Minneapolis, Minnesota. More than seven in ten Native Americans now live in metropolitan areas.

In the 1950s, many Indigenous people moved to cities. Some came by choice because they wanted to start a new life, or to make money, or to experience something different. Others were encouraged by the U.S. government's Indian Termination Policy, which offered money to Indigenous people who were willing to give up their tribal identities.

The plan was to gradually solve the "Indian problem" by disappearing Indigenous people, their cultures, and languages until there were no more Indians.

The Indian Termination Policy didn't work. People from different tribes ended up in the same cities, and now, two or three generations later, they have forged relationships with one another and put down roots in cities across the country.

with these images because discussing where we are going requires that we know where we came from.

From there, the story jumps from character to character. Among them are Opal Bear Shield and Jacquie Red Feather. For Opal and Jacquie, home in the city used to be a locked station wagon in an empty parking lot.

One of Jacquie's grandsons is fourteen-year-old Orvil Red Feather. He spends hours in his bedroom trying on regalia that is too small for him. He depends on YouTube to learn about Indigenous practices. (Tommy shares that he sometimes clicks on YouTube too.)

And then there is Tony Loneman, who is twenty-one. He was born with fetal alcohol syndrome (he calls it the "Drome") and he deals drugs.

Nobody who reads *There There* will forget the characters or the shocking ending. Tommy accomplished what he'd set out to do: he made urban Indigenous people visible.

Tommy Orange took six years to finish *There There*. Once it was published, it quickly became a bestseller. The reviews were sensational, and Tommy became a literary star. The *San Francisco Chronicle* wrote: "Exquisite . . . [An] exceptional debut . . . Sublimely render[s] the truth of experiences that are passed over."

Tommy is working to bring along the next generation of Indigenous writers. He teaches at the Institute of American Indian Arts, where he received a master of fine arts degree himself. He can teach his students how to navigate the process of getting published, but most of his work focuses on how to write. He believes that writing well is not mysterious. A good musician practices and practices and practices, and it's the same for writing. His goal is to keep telling stories. One of the things he loves about writing and reading is the feeling you get when you read something and think, "I didn't know anybody else thought that."

Author Tommy Orange speaks during the Believer Festival in 2019 in Las Vegas, Nevada.

Tidal salt marsh on Cape Breton Island, Nova Scotia, land of the Mi'kmaq

Chapter 7

RITA JOE
Finds Her Talk
Mi'kmaq, 1932–2007

Rita Joe was a poet, storyteller, residential school survivor, and a gentle fighter for the Mi'kmaq way of life. Though she knew hard times, her poems are full of hope. She shows us how to heal without letting the past make us bitter.

I Lost My Talk

I lost my talk
The talk you took away
When I was a little girl
At Shubenacadie school.

You snatched it away;
I speak like you
I think like you
I create like you
The scrambled ballad, about my word.

Two ways I talk
Both ways I say,
Your way is more powerful.

So gently I offer my hand and ask,
Let me find my talk
So I can teach you about me.

RITA JOE WAS BORN INTO A Mi'kmaw community in Whycocomagh, Cape Breton, Nova Scotia. She knew a lot of heartache when she was young. Her mother, Annie, a weaver of beautiful baskets, died when Rita was only five years old. Her father, Joseph, a carver of fine wooden axe handles, died when she was ten. Now orphaned, Rita lived in a string of foster homes. "I would stay for six months, maybe three months, maybe a year, two months, a month, two weeks," she wrote in her autobiography. Some of the foster homes were good. Others were awful. In one, her foster mother even put her to work making moonshine. Alcohol-fueled beatings made every day a torment.

Twelve-year-old Rita decided to take charge of her life. She wrote to the Indian Agent and asked to go to the Shubenacadie Indian Residential School. She would get away from her foster parents, and she'd learn to cook and sew so that she would never have to rely on anyone to take care of her.

When Rita first saw the big brick school, she thought it looked like a castle. She wasn't at the school for long before she thought it was more like a prison. She had to do everything according to a mind-numbing schedule. She had no say in when she ate, when she prayed, or even when she went to the bathroom. Her Mi'kmaw language was forbidden. She had to live every day in English. The message was clear, as she once told a CBC Radio interviewer: "I was brainwashed. 'You're no good,' I was told every day at Shubie."

Rita stayed at the school for four years. At sixteen, she headed to Halifax armed with a Grade 8 education, one change of clothes, and a few dollars in her pocket. She loved her freedom, or as much freedom as she could hope for in 1948, even though she worked twelve-hour days at the Halifax Infirmary. With her first paycheck she bought a pair of red shoes. That was Rita's way of announcing to the world that she was ready for adventure.

Rita worked hard and fell in love a lot. She became a single mother at seventeen. Realizing that she had no way to support her baby, she gave the child to her sister Annabel to raise. Soon she was pregnant again. This time she took a train to Boston, Massachusetts, to find better work and start a new life with her baby.

In Boston Rita met and married Frank Joe. His family was from Eskasoni, the largest reserve in Atlantic Canada, and he planned to return there. Though Rita had never been to Eskasoni, she felt right at home. Once again, she could live speaking Mi'kmaq. She quickly relearned the traditions her parents had taught her long ago.

Though Rita grew to love Eskasoni, her troubles weren't over. The marriage that began with so much hope turned into an abusive one. For years Rita put up with Frank's many girlfriends, his drinking, and his beatings. Eventually she found her voice. "I began to run away from home for

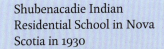

Shubenacadie Indian Residential School in Nova Scotia in 1930

periods of time. I would live with friends and relatives and tell my story to anyone who would listen."

Writing helped Rita make sense of her life. She'd scribbled her first poem on a scrap of paper when she was just seven. Now she began to carve out time to write. She wrote a poem that was published in the *Micmac News* in 1969. It led to her writing a monthly column, "Here and There in Eskasoni." She talked to the older people in the community and wrote down their stories. Her writing inspired a flood of feedback, some negative but most of it encouraging. The more she wrote, the more confident she became. Rita's great gift was that she never tried to cover over her painful memories, but she didn't let them define her either. Writing helped her face them.

Rita and Frank had eight children and eventually raised foster children too. Her older children began to come home from school with reports of racism and learning twisted histories about Indigenous people. Rita listened to their stories and read their textbooks. The one-sided history taught to children upset her, and she vowed to correct it.

Rita realized that by writing about the Mi'kmaq, she was telling her story.

"I began to write beautiful stories using poetry. I don't know why poetry because I was not a poet. But in poetry you have to use beautiful words sometimes. And that's what I did. I tried to write beautiful stuff about Native culture."

Her first book, *Poems of Rita Joe,* was published in 1978. It was met with a flood of gratitude from people who saw themselves in her poems. When people told her that they were touched by her honest telling of her experiences as a Mi'kmaw woman, all she said was, "I'm just stating the facts of life."

Poetry made Rita famous. The little girl who had to make moonshine in a

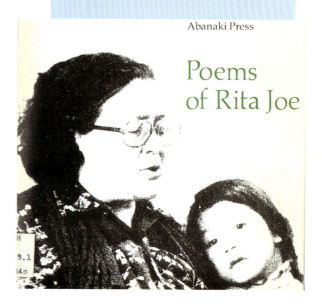

Cover of the book Rita Joe published in 1978, *Poems of Rita Joe*

brutal foster home grew up to receive many awards and honorary degrees. Dressed in her traditional deerskin dress, she met the prime minister and the Queen of England, and always remained a proud Mi'kmaw woman.

Her success and recognition inspired her to learn more, share more, write more. She wrote seven books in all, including *Poems of Rita Joe* (1978), *Song of Eskasoni* (1988), and *The Blind Man's Eyes*, which was published in 2015, after she died.

Rita's homelife, once so difficult, turned into a love story in the end. Her husband Frank stopped drinking and went back to school, earning degrees in teaching and sociology. His abuse ended. "In the last years of our life together, there was so much love given and expressed between us," she said.

Frank died in 1989, when Rita was fifty-seven. A year later, she developed Parkinson's disease, an illness that causes tremors and difficulty with coordination. "I tremble like an aspen leaf," she wrote.

Rita wrote until the end of her life. Blind in one eye, almost deaf, and wearing mismatching socks, she sat at her typewriter picking out letters with one finger because her left hand shook. Her last works were mostly songs. She had always liked to make up tunes, and now her melodies and her words came together. One of her greatest pleasures was to hear her Christmas songs sung in English and Mi'kmaq.

She died in 2007, but her legacy is everywhere. She used to tell her children that after she was gone her words would still exist. They are part of history now.

The day Rita died, there was a page left in her typewriter with a finished poem.

Mi'kmaq poet Rita Joe is invested into the Order of Canada in 1989 by Governor General Ray Hnatyshyn, in a ceremony at Rideau Hall, Ottawa, Canada.

Prime Minister Justin Trudeau and Métis Nation president Clément Chartier meet in Ottawa, Canada, in April 2017, when the Canada-Métis Nation Accord was signed.

Chapter 8

MARILYN DUMONT'S
Métis Voice
Métis, b. 1955

> Writing has saved my emotional, spiritual, and intellectual life in a country where I wasn't supposed to exist, let alone thrive . . . It allows a space for my sense of self.
>
> —Marilyn Dumont

PART 3 | Our History Is in Our Poems, Songs, and Written Stories

MARILYN DUMONT IS A POET who uses her pen to tell readers about her Métis culture and history. Like Pauline Johnson once did, she writes poetry to challenge the stereotypes and expectations that society places on Indigenous women. Marilyn has gathered her poems into books such as *A Really Good Brown Girl* (1996) and *The Pemmican Eaters* (2015) that have received many awards. Although she experienced many changes in her life, poetry has been her passion since she was a teenager. Now in her sixties, she can look back with joy on the recognition she has earned.

Marilyn is also a successful, modern woman. She is a professor in the Department of English at the University of Alberta, in Edmonton, where she teaches creative writing. She uses her position to teach a younger generation to channel their passion for poetry into words that call attention to the topics that matter to them.

It is a long way from the poverty of her youth. Marilyn's early life was not easy. Her family carried the burden of history that came with their surname.

When she started school, Marilyn Dumont found the study of Canadian history difficult because of what she had to learn. She was born in 1955, and even as a young girl growing up in the late 1950s in Olds, a small town in Alberta, she sensed that her family was different because of the way people treated them.

In history class, her teachers told her stories of her Métis ancestry that troubled her. One had to do with the name Dumont. Gabriel Dumont had led a rebellion against the government of Canada. For that, he was branded a traitor. People

Cover of *The Pemmican Eaters*, the award-winning collection of poems by Marilyn Dumont

Louis Riel as photographed around 1873

spoke bitter words about Marilyn and her family and resented their presence. Their neighbors treated them like outcasts who deserved to live on an unpaved road allowance at the edge of town.

At home, Marilyn learned a different version of the story. Her parents talked about the roots of her Métis family that began with Jean-Baptiste Dumont. He had traveled west with the fur trade in the 1790s for the North West Company. He was at a trading post near where the city of Edmonton, Alberta, stands today, when he met and married Josephte Sarcee, a Tsuut'ina woman whose people went there to trade. Their children were the ancestors of today's Métis people. One of their descendants, Gabriel Dumont, was a Métis hero. He was a renowned buffalo hunter, a champion of Métis rights, and a brave leader during the North-West Resistance of 1885.

Marilyn grew up poor. Her parents had no money to spend on books. Apart from newspapers there was nothing to read in the house. But at the age of sixteen, and despite being a quiet student, Marilyn read out loud a poem she wrote for a class. That day she discovered the power of words.

School was never her favorite place. Nobody tried to stop her when she decided to drop out in Grade 10. Leaving

Gabriel Dumont, military commander of the Métis during the North-West Resistance of 1885

school meant freedom. She got married when she was seventeen and didn't have much time for writing. But she was eager to learn and went back to school when she was twenty-five, the first person in her family to attend university.

At university Marilyn learned to understand and challenge the colonial history she studied in grade school. She wanted to tell the real story of her people—a story that historians had ignored or twisted.

Marilyn chose poetry as her way to tell the Métis story. Since then, her mission has been to use words in ways that challenge people to think. Her contribution to the name Dumont is to make it mean more than just a rebel. Now it also means poet.

Many obstacles got in her way, but from her struggles came the inspiration for her poems. In her first book, *A Really Good Brown Girl,* she described her experiences with racism that no child should have to face. Her readers discovered a Métis woman whose words carried a sense of urgency after being silent for too long.

Since then, every book she's written draws on the experiences that have made her the person she is. Through her poetry she contests the lessons she once studied to seek the true history about herself and her people. Most of all, she wants the world to know that she, her family, and her people exist.

A Métis scarf being woven by weaver Pris Lepine, a Chipewyan/Métis from Fort Smith, Northwest Territories

In the poem "All rags now," she gives us a snapshot of Métis life as seen through her eyes:

once inside - tiny moth's wings
warmed to a hot bulb   fire-catching kindling
spirit-cracked pot   frozen plywood floor   burnt toast cast iron-hot
toes cold   tummy turning rags   hands shivering   yet, fingers of light underfoot
melt ice-hard days   hard kernel of rag rugs   previous lives turning
Aunt Bessie's fiddle-playing blouse   Sam's only-dress-pants   Moises' white shirt
all rags, now   cut-bearing you   braiding long rope-bending lives   over-around-over
around   Dosey Doe your partner   all rag days, now   ripped
scent of tobacco & hand soap   in the fold-shreds   an old house coat   torn new lives
hold patchwork   a place to stand   walk ahead, nitanis, walk
to another time   recall these threads   these stitches
you will as you leave this road   allowance & you will as   you ride those rags of light,

ride those rags of light rags of light.

Who Are the Métis?

A narrow definition of "Métis" means a person of mixed ancestry. However, it can also refer to the Métis Nation, which is a community of people with a distinct history and way of life. First Nations, Inuit, and Métis are recognized as Aboriginal people in Canada's Constitution Act (1982).

Although the Red River country in southern Manitoba has the largest Métis population and the most history, Métis communities formed around fur trading posts. The Métis Nation became a political force in 1816 when Cuthbert Grant rallied his warriors against the settlers at the Battle of Seven Oaks, as the British had instructed the Hudson's Bay Company to encourage white settlement of land near its trading posts. But the Métis were living on the land. For the next seventy years, until the North-West Resistance ended in 1885, the Métis fought battles to resist the violence they endured. Hundreds of people died, and the resistance was eventually crushed by federal troops. Their leader, Louis Riel, was captured, put on trial, and hanged.

Chapter 9

JAY ODJICK
Tells a Superhero Story
Zibi Anishinabeg

Jay Odjick is wild about comics. Ever since he can remember he has devoured everything he can find about superheroes. When he was small, the only thing he couldn't find in the comic books he read was himself. He knew he would have loved to read about an Anishinaabeg superhero, so he invented one: Kagagi, the Raven. He created this character mainly to entertain, but also to teach readers about Anishinaabeg culture and language.

IN ANISHINAABEG TRADITION, Raven is a powerful figure with the ability to transform the world. He's a trickster, sometimes selfish, sometimes mischievous, and always hungry. His special superpower is his clever mind.

Matthew Carver is an ordinary teenager, and his problems are all the usual high school drama. That is, until the day he learns that he has inherited an ancient power—and the responsibility that comes with it. An age-old monster is prowling the world once more. Windigo is an evil being that eats human flesh. People who are possessed by Windigo become cannibals. Matthew must unleash his power to defeat him. Matthew isn't an average kid anymore. He is now Kagagi, the Raven.

Kagagi, the Raven became an animated TV show in the United States, Canada, and Australia. Jay Odjick was the lead writer, executive producer, and lead designer. While children are the main audience, an elderly man once told Jay that he watched the show because it was his only chance to hear his own language. This remark touched Jay, and he realized that, like his character, he too has responsibilities with his creations.

For as long as he can remember Jay was the kid with the sketchbook who only wanted to write and draw. Down the street from his home in Rochester, New York, a shop sold comic books. Shopkeepers are supposed to let

A poster created to promote *Kagagii, the Raven*, both a comic book series and an animated TV show

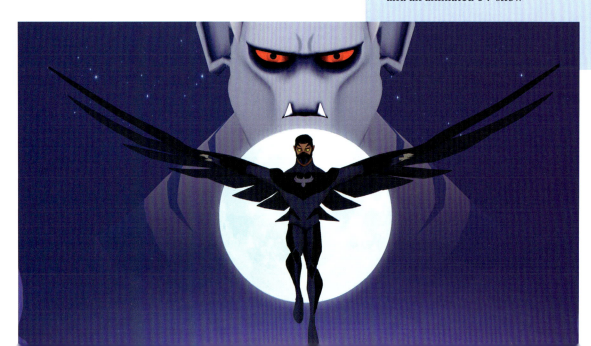

Jay Odjick's obsession with comic books started at a very early age, continued throughout his twenties and lasted into adulthood.

publishers know which comics or magazines didn't sell by sending back the covers and throwing away the inside pages. This shopkeeper would tear off the covers, but he sold the contents to kids for five cents each. Jay was hooked.

Jay's father left the Kitigan Zibi Anishinabeg community in Quebec at the age of thirteen. But when he started a family of his own, he didn't want to raise them in their poor, tough neighborhood in Rochester. Seeing the yellow chalk outline of a murder victim staining the sidewalk near their home wasn't unusual, so when Jay was five, the family moved back to his father's community, just outside Maniwaki.

Jay didn't lose his obsession with comic books. He was very young when he plotted out his own superhero comics. At first, Jay told the stories, and he paid his friends to draw the images. He had clear ideas of what he wanted the superheroes to look like, and he picked apart his friends' art. Fed up, they told him to draw what he wanted himself.

From the time he fell in love with comics he had always looked to see who had written and drawn them. Now it was his turn. By the time he was ten he had his first rejection letter. It was from Marvel Comics, a major publisher. It didn't discourage him one bit. Just the opposite. He is a person who loves a challenge: "I took my craft seriously. I bought anatomy books and books about perspectives then sat down and had to figure it all out."

Though school was never his passion, Jay graduated from high school and had plans to go on to college. He was living in a rundown neighborhood. One day, the roof of the house collapsed. Jay found himself homeless and had to look for work right away. Nobody expected him to make a living by creating comics, but he was determined to try.

The comic book world is tough to break into. For an Indigenous artist there are even more barriers. Comic bookstores told him that nobody wanted to read about Indigenous characters. Eventually a computer programmer friend gave him a hand to create a *webtoon*, or cartoon for the Internet. For two years Jay learned web design and drew comics as a full-time job before he started his own business. He didn't know how to create a business plan, but he figured that if others could do it, so could he. He got a small loan and set up his own publishing company.

All day he worked on the business and at night he wrote and drew comics. By luck, one day he went to a convention and found himself in the booth next to the publisher of Arcana Comics, one of the most important comic publishers in Canada. Arcana became his publisher and finally Jay could focus on his art.

Jay has also become well known as a picture-book illustrator, especially for his work with children's author Robert Munsch. *Blackflies*, published in 2017, is about a girl named Helen who must save her sister who has been carried away by blackflies. *Bear for Breakfast* (Makwa kidji

Jay Odjick experiemented with digital painting, as seen in this example titled *Spirit of the Forest*.

kijebà wìsiniyàn), published two years later, is about a boy who decides to catch a bear to eat for breakfast, just like his grandfather.

Though he is at home with modern graphic novels and comics, and animation for television, he respects traditions he learned from his grandfather and his grandmother, a medicine woman as well as a teacher. His grandparents are the ones who taught Jay about Windigo and his nemesis Kagagi, the Raven.

He puts that respect into action by working to keep the Algonquin language alive. For years he has posted an Algonquin Word of the Day on Twitter (now called X). And he's proud that there are three versions of the Kagagi series—one in English, one with 20 percent Algonquin, and one that is entirely in Algonquin. *Bear for Breakfast* is published in Algonquin, English, and French.

Adaptation to the modern, high-tech world is just as important as tradition to Jay. He uses his own community as an example. It was founded by about a dozen families who hunted for food. Now there are thousands of people on the same amount of land. If everyone still lived off hunting, they would soon clear out the whole deer population, so they have adapted to a new way of life. He says, "We need to define who we are as native people because the world has changed." He realized the world was always changing and so were his people. He doesn't want Indigenous kids to be left behind. He believes that they deserve to find their best lives with what they have today.

Jay has a message for kids: "You have a voice that nobody can replicate. If you sing your songs, no one can take that away from you. Emulating is fine, but you must use your own voice and learn to do things your way. Share the way you look at the world, because no one can see things the way you do."

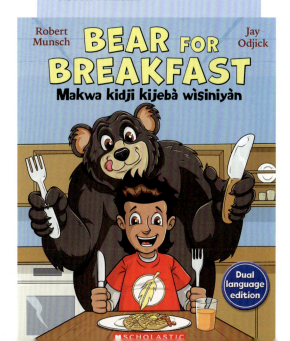

Jay Odjick illustrated the cover of the picture book *Bear for Breakfast*, written by famed children's writer Robert Munsch.

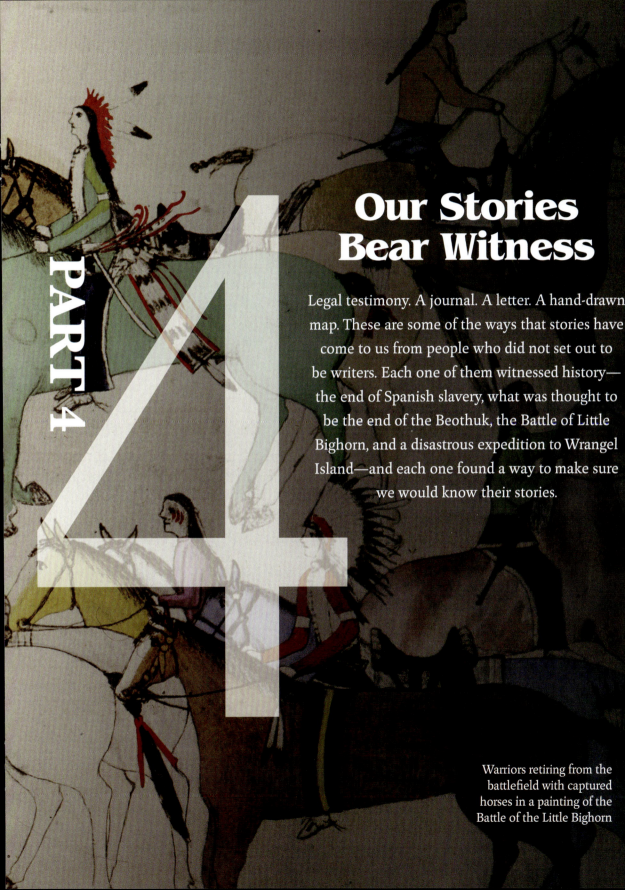

PART 4

Our Stories Bear Witness

Legal testimony. A journal. A letter. A hand-drawn map. These are some of the ways that stories have come to us from people who did not set out to be writers. Each one of them witnessed history—the end of Spanish slavery, what was thought to be the end of the Beothuk, the Battle of Little Bighorn, and a disastrous expedition to Wrangel Island—and each one found a way to make sure we would know their stories.

Warriors retiring from the battlefield with captured horses in a painting of the Battle of the Little Bighorn

From the *Conquest of Mexico* series by the Spanish School, the taking of Tenochtitlan by Hernán Cortéz in 1521

BEATRIZ AND CATALINA

Chapter 10

Court Records Tell Their Story

Maya, c. 1516

Leaving a record of your story is possible even if you can't read or write. Enslaved people like Beatriz and her daughter Catalina found the incredible courage to sue the men who claimed to be their masters. The transcripts of their trials are more than five hundred years old now, yet the bravery of these two women and their court battles still inspire those who seek justice today.

SHORT, THIN, AND MISSING A tooth, Beatriz was only fourteen when Spanish slave traders kidnapped her and forced her onto a ship bound for Lisbon, Portugal. She would never see her home in Mexico again. Though she was just a child herself, she was about to have a baby. She must have been bewildered and terrified.

When Christopher Columbus landed in what he called Hispaniola in 1492 he expected to find precious spices and gold to take back to the King and Queen of Spain. He found no gold or jewels, so he captured Indigenous people to give as "gifts" to those who had funded his voyage. In the years that followed at least 650,000 people from Florida, the Caribbean islands, Venezuela, and Mexico were enslaved by the Spanish. Beatriz was one of them.

Men enslaved by the Spanish were usually put to work in Mexican silver mines or in Caribbean sugarcane fields. Most women and children were shipped across the Atlantic to Spain in the belief they were better suited for domestic work in Spanish homes.

Spain passed the New Laws in 1542, forbidding taking new slaves from the lands they had colonized. (The New Laws also stated that Indigenous people couldn't be forced to carry loads against their will, and they couldn't be forced to dive for pearls.) The exception was if an Indigenous man protested Spanish abuse or rebelled against Spanish colonists; then he and his

Detail from a painting depicting the arrival of the Spanish conquistador Hernán Cortés at Vera Cruz

wife and children could be seized and sold. However, enslaving people living in lands that other nations had claimed remained legal. The New Laws would change the course of Beatriz's life.

In 1538 a merchant visiting Lisbon, Portugal, bought Beatriz and her baby son, Simon, and sold them to Juan Cansino, an important man in Carmona, Spain. Juan was a harsh master. Beatriz's chores never ended. She swept the floors, washed clothes, prepared food, and looked after Juan's children. Weary days—then months and years—passed with no relief from drudgery.

Over the years, Beatriz had five more children. All were born into slavery in Juan's home. Her oldest daughter was Catalina. By the time she was seventeen, Catalina had tried many times to escape, and urged her brothers to do the same. As punishment, Juan sold Simon and branded Catalina's face.

Beatriz swore that she and her children would be free. All she had to do was prove that she had come from Mexico, land that the Spanish had conquered. She took a courageous, risky step: she sued the powerful and cruel Juan Cansino.

As soon as Juan Cansino learned of the lawsuit, he became even more vicious.

Beatriz had no choice but to continue living under his roof, so Juan had plenty of time to direct his anger at her.

Finally, the day of the trial came. Beatriz took her place in front of the judges. Softly, she spoke: "I [Beatriz] am from Mexico City in New Spain and for more than twenty years Juan Cansino,

The New Laws of the Indies were meant to protect the Indigenous inhabitants of lands owned by the Spanish Crown.

magistrate of the village of Carmona, has held me and my six children captive, he [even] sold one of them. Because he is the magistrate and favored in the village of Carmona, I have not been able to attain justice."

Beatriz's lawyer was Gregorio López. In the year after the New Laws were passed, he had launched sixteen lawsuits on behalf of slaves. He thought that Beatriz's case would be straightforward. All he had to prove was that Beatriz was from Mexico.

But Beatriz couldn't answer questions about Mexico. She had been gone for so long, she had forgotten the language she spoke when she was a little girl and almost everything else about her home. Juan argued that the New Laws didn't apply to her, claiming she was an Arab, and that she was from the Portuguese Indies.

Juan explained away branding Catalina by saying that she deserved the punishment. After all, she had run away from him many times. He claimed that she had stolen his wheat, cheese, wine, and wool. As for Simon, Juan said that he had sold him because he was a thief, and

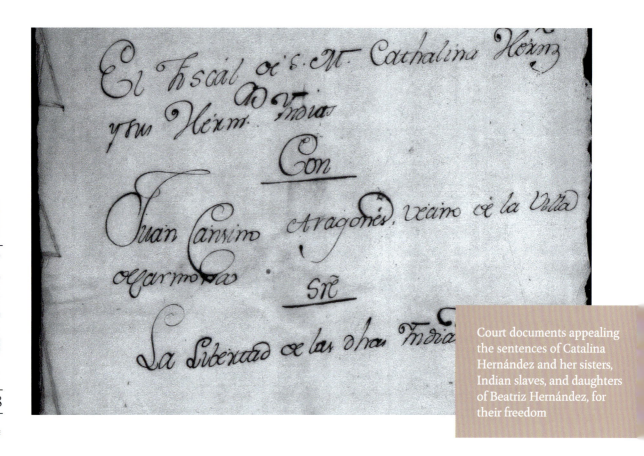

Court documents appealing the sentences of Catalina Hernández and her sisters, Indian slaves, and daughters of Beatriz Hernández, for their freedom

Yo fran[cisco] de diguiez s[criv]ano de su mag[estad] y lugarten[ient]e de escr[ivano]
de la casa del a[u]on[?]a[?]on de las yndias doy fe a v[uest]ra m[erce]d
de s[eñ]or q[ue] estan[do] p[ar]a esc[ucha]r trata[do] e siguiendo[se]
tienda dela d[ic]ha casa ante los s[eñor]es juezes officiales
p[re]sid[en]tes della v[n]a . fran[cisco] sar[mient]o p[rocur]ador del[os yndios]
en n[ombr]e y en dem[and]a pr[ocur]ador general delos yndios en
n[ombr]e de Catalina hernandez e Juan[?] sanch[ez]
hermanos y Juana su hija yndios a v[uestr]a d[ema]n[d]ante
sobre la libertad dellos e dela otra j[uan] canano[?] u[e]z[ino]
aragones y dela v[e]z[inda]d de Carmona elqual sien[do]
v[i]st[o] los p[a]resc[e] que los d[ic]hos s[eño]res juezes llegar nueva[ment]e
adj[u]nta sen tena dela qual p[or] p[ar]te del d[ic]ho f[rancisco]
sar[mient]o f[u]e apelad[o] p[ar]a ante su mag[estad] e los s[eñores] del
su Real consejo delas Yndias e ya no della qual
d[ic]ha sentenç[i]a se dio en effecto que se sigue

En el pl[eit]o que es entre el p[rocurad]or de la una f[ranciso]
sar[mient]o pr[ocur]ador general delos yndios en n[om]b[re]
de Catalina Hernandez y sus hermanos e Juana
su hija yndios actor demandante su libertad dellos
e de la otra demanda[do] Joan can[s]ino aragones
u[e]z[in]o de la v[ez]i[nda]d de Carmona amo delos d[ichos] yndios
e defendiente e en n[om]b[re] del ser [ean]cansino su hijo
e gonçalo de molina pr[ocur]ador delas n[onc]as[?]
esta casa v[i]stos los aut[os] e m[eri]tos deste proces[o]

Fallamos que el [?] fran[cisco] sar[mient]o en n[om]b[r]e

what's more, he was "mischievous."

Beatriz lost the suit. The verdict broke her. With the lawsuit done, she had to spend the rest of her life back in Juan's household.

Thirteen years passed. Beatriz was dead. Juan was an old man. His son Ferdinand ran the household. Even after all those long years, Catalina was still rebellious. During the spring of 1572, when Catalina was in her early thirties and had a ten-year-old daughter of her own, she spoke with lawyers. She explained that her mother had been an uneducated woman who had been a child when she was enslaved. Beatriz couldn't defend herself in a trial, but Catalina could.

She wrote out a long list of witnesses who could swear that Beatriz had come from Mexico. Juan's lawyers threatened and insulted Catalina's witnesses. They described one witness, Isabel Navarra, as "a person belonging to a lowly race with no fixed opinions who was untrustworthy because she is a morisca" (descended from Moors). Juan's lawyers dismissed Marianna, another witness, saying, "She is Indian and as such would lie in order to favor Catalina, and as an Indian, she is a lowly person."

Both sides fought hard, but once again the rich and powerful Juan Cansino won. Catalina, her brothers and sisters, and her young daughter remained enslaved. But she wasn't done. She appealed her case and two years later, the ruling was overturned. Forty years had passed since Beatriz was dragged onto a Spanish ship, but finally her children and grandchild were free.

Word spread quickly about Indigenous people who were willing to tell their stories to the courts. By 1550 even those who were living in small towns and villages were aware that they were entitled to be free. Despite the favorable court rulings, slavery continued in Spain until it was outlawed in the early seventeenth century. All because Beatriz, Catalina, and other enslaved people risked beatings and torture to tell their stories.

Opposite: An anonymous painting from the eighteenth century showing sixteen racial groupings

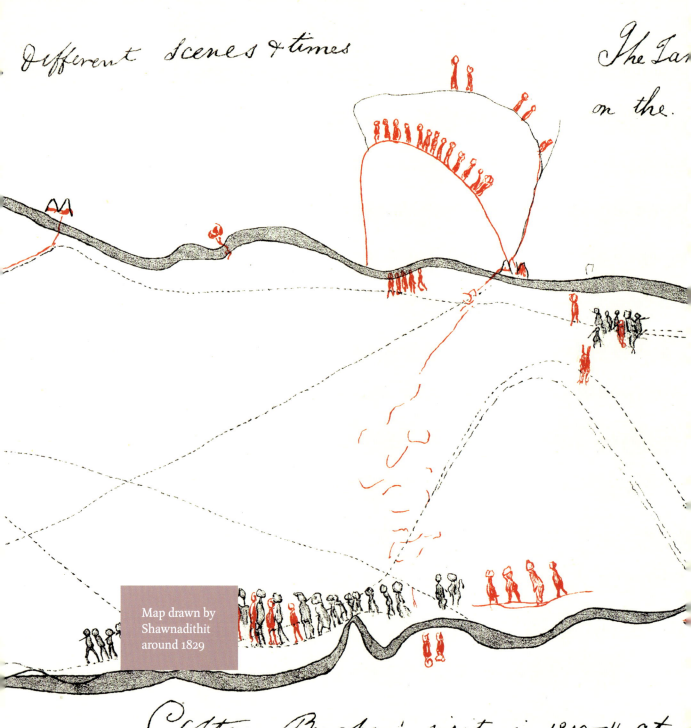

Chapter 11

SHAWNADITHIT
Maps Her Story
Beothuk, c. 1800–1829

Shawnadithit lived a short, hard life. Her people, the Beothuk, were in danger of being wiped out from disease and violence that came with white settlers. The maps she drew recorded what she saw—including murder.

THE ISLAND HAD BEEN Beothuk land for at least two thousand years when English and French settlers arrived and named it Newfoundland. By the time Shawnadithit was born around 1800, the Beothuk population had dwindled to a few hundred.

As the settlers took over more and more land, the Beothuk were forced inland. Without access to the coast where they used to hunt and fish, they faced starvation. Many died from the diseases brought by Europeans, especially tuberculosis. Others died by violence. In the 1820s Henry Bathurst, Britain's secretary of state for the colonies, realized that the Beothuk, wary of the settlers, tried to hide from them. He wrote:

> **"There was reason to believe that our people had frequently put them to death without sufficient provocation, and in some instances, I am ashamed to say, they were shot at in mere sport."**

Shawnadithit saw much of this. In 1819 she was at Red Indian Lake when fur traders captured her aunt Demasduit. Her uncle, Chief Nonosabasut, and his brother tried to rescue Demasduit. The two men were killed on the spot. Demasduit's newborn baby died the next day. When Demasduit died a year later, Shawnadithit watched as the English brought her aunt's body back to the deserted encampment.

In 1823 Shawnadithit and her mother and sister were starving and sick when they too were captured by English fur traders. They were taken to the city of St. John's, where the English gave them some medical care and gifts to take back to their people as a goodwill gesture. Then they dumped the women by the Bay of Exploits. There was little game to hunt, and soon they were starving again. Her mother and sister got sicker and died. Shawnadithit was taken into the home of John Peyton Jr., a merchant at Exploits. He gave her an English name, Nance, or Nancy April. John was the very person in charge of the mission that had led to the kidnapped Demasduit and the murdered Nonosabasut.

The English thought that the Beothuk way of life might disappear. By some estimates there were now only twenty people left, so in 1827 an Englishman named William Epps Cormack set up the Beothuk Institution in St. John's to preserve their culture. He asked Shawnadithit to record information about her language and

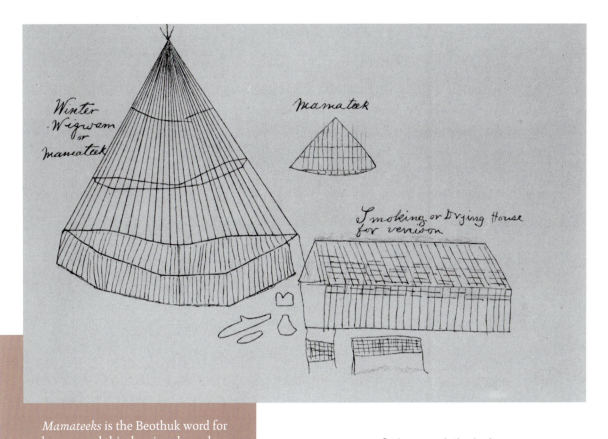

Mamateeks is the Beothuk word for houses, and this drawing shows how summer and winter ones were built.

practices. She drew maps and pictures of everyday items and taught him several Beothuk words.

Only a dozen of Shawnadithit's drawings survive today. They give us a glimpse of her world. She drew a neat store house where they stacked birch bark boxes of dried venison, or deer meat for their winter food supply. She drew water buckets from different angles. One detailed drawing shows a figure in a tunic and skirt.

Five of Shawnadithit's drawings are mental maps that represent the geographical knowledge she held in her mind. They tell her stories. One map shows the heavily armed British settlers capturing her aunt and the spot where they killed Nonosabasut. In red pencil to symbolize blood, she marked the routes that her family took when they fled from the settlers who were armed with muskets and bayonets.

She shows us the spot near the lake where fur traders captured Demasduit and killed her husband and where their newborn baby died. The drawing also shows the long trek the English made the following January carrying the pine coffin containing Demasduit's body back to the lake where they had kidnapped her. Shawnadithit drew her memory of the spot where her aunt, next to her husband and their baby, were buried together. She marked in red the places where her family hid from the English. She drew the route they took back to the lake. And one map is supposed to show their last encampment.

Shawnadithit lived in William's household for five years before he went back to England. She never saw him again. Six years after her capture, she died of tuberculosis in 1829 at the age of about thirty.

History called Shawnadithit the last Beothuk, but a new story is emerging from samples of ancient DNA—a shorthand way of saying "deoxyribonucleic acid." It's the genetic information, a kind of code, that makes us who we are. Geneticists can search for Beothuk lineage by comparing genomes in modern populations, for example, with hair taken from Shawnadithit's hairbrush. According to Mi'kmaw oral histories, when the Beothuk fled their island homeland, they intermarried with mainland people. The Mi'kmaq of Miawpukek First Nation have begun DNA research of their own to see whether the Beothuk lineages are present in their community.

Mapping Our Story

Indigenous people are remapping and renaming their lands, bringing together art and interactive technology. The result is "creative narrative cartography," or story mapping. The Zuni live in western New Mexico. Jim Enote, the director of the A:shiwi A:wan Museum, is involved in "counter mapping." He wanted an atlas that represented the Zuni worldview, so he invited several tribal artists to produce maps of their homeland. The artists challenged ideas about mapping. North doesn't have to be "up," for instance. Scale can have to do with what's important to a traveler, like the number of sleeps to their destination, not distance in miles or kilometers.

This drawing by John Cartwright from around 1773 is titled *Beothuk Camp with Canoe*.

Opposite: The sculpture *Spirit of the Beothuk* is found in the community of Boyd's Cove, Newfoundland and Labrador.

Below: Shawnadithit's drawings representing a variety of subjects such as cups and spears

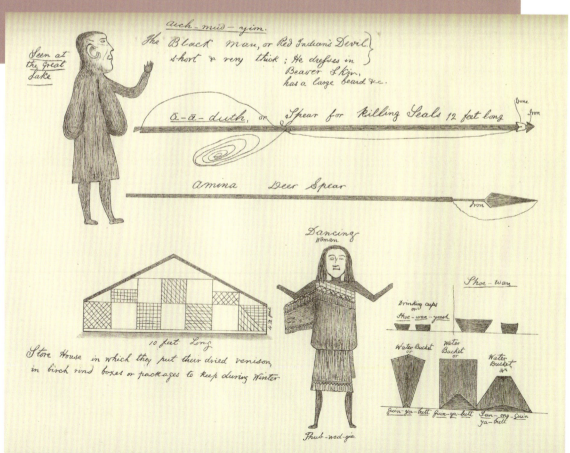

Oglala Sioux women on horseback in 1907

Chapter 12

STANDING BEAR
Warrior Witness
Oglala Sioux, 1859–c. 1935

The battle known as Custer's Last Stand is a popular topic for songs, books, and movies. Certainly, none of Custer's men left a record. They all died that day. The only reliable eyewitness reports come from Sioux warriors who were in the fight. Standing Bear is one of those eyewitnesses who made history. In a letter he describes what happened when his people were attacked by the U.S. army.

SETTLERS CLAIMED THE prairie land and wanted to get rid of the Indigenous people who lived there. Tribes were offered treaties and reservations to live on. If they objected, the U.S. army was sent to fight them.

In 1875 the army sent out General George Armstrong Custer, along with a thousand soldiers, scouts, and reporters, to find a place to build a fort. Custer brought back news of gold in the country that was promised to the Lakota by treaties. The government tried to buy the Black Hills, but Lakota leaders refused to sell.

Chiefs such as Sitting Bull and Crazy Horse vowed to keep colonists off their land. "We want no white men here," Sitting Bull declared. "The Black Hills belong to me. If the whites try to take them, I will fight."

The time to fight came soon. U.S. troops were dispatched to chase the Sioux onto reservations. Sitting Bull sent runners to all the camps, calling his people to meet for a Sun Dance at the Rosebud River. By spring 1876, thousands of Sioux

Warriors Standing Bear and White Eagle

General George Armstrong Custer was sent by the U.S. government to move the Sioux onto reservations.

and Cheyenne warriors answered the call. Early that summer Sitting Bull's camp was the largest in Lakota history; there were at least fourteen hundred lodges.

Six weeks passed. More people joined Sitting Bull's camp, bringing the numbers up to about seven thousand people, including eighteen hundred men and boys who could fight. There were so many people that they had to keep moving to provide enough food for their horses. On June 24, they had settled on the banks of the river they called the Greasy Grass, the one soldiers knew as the Little Bighorn.

Standing Bear was one of the young Lakota men who had answered Sitting Bull's call. Many years later, he described what happened in a letter to a friend:

I was probably seventeen or eighteen years old when my uncle told me we would have a Sun Dance near the Rosebud River that Sitting Bull [had called] and many Indians would attend. I watched them dance for three or four days without eating anything or drinking water. Some of them had sick wives or children and asked Sitting Bull to heal them.

The next day we moved from the Rosebud River to Greasy Grass River where our people had a fight with the soldiers. Five of our people were shot but I did not see any of this. The next day we moved on and remained there for two days. The third day we moved to a river where all the others had set up their tepees. It was a large group. The following morning my mother, my aunt and my siblings got up early to look for wild turnips and many men went hunting. My uncle asked me to fetch the horses and water them. I went swimming first.

Then I heard a man shouting that the soldiers were coming. They had shot a boy that was on his way to get our horses. I ran back and saw that another man was bringing our horses, I sprang onto a horse, but didn't have time to dress, I had only my shirt but no shoes. I rode with my uncle in the direction toward Major Reno [one of the U.S. army leaders] when on the hill we saw Custer advancing. Before we got closer, we saw hundreds upon hundreds of our people around us. A few of them had guns and most of them had bows and arrows. I saw a few of ours bleeding, lying on the ground.

Then I saw the soldiers let their horses run to the river. I wanted to catch one of them but there were too many ahead of me, even so I saw some soldiers heading for the river, but they did not get too far and although they ran in different directions two of them were shot immediately. The third one had run quite a distance when one of our men cried out to let him go, but someone had already shot him. I think that they were all dead. I think it is a lie that a Crow Indian was ever in Custer's fight.

After Custer's fight we rode toward [Major] Reno. I stayed until evening; the powder dust and the blood made me sick. The next day we rode toward Reno but I did not stay very long because my siblings were young and I wanted to help my mother. Toward evening we moved on because we heard that more soldiers were coming . . .

I do not know if Sitting Bull was in the battle. Since his tepee was not in our area, I did not see him. But I did see him in the Sun Dance and send you the picture. A year after the battle he moved to Canada where I saw him again after Crazy Horse died.

All of our people wanted to know why some of the whites wanted to drive us out of the Black Hills. He knew that there were forests, animals, and gold [in the hills] and the white people wanted these riches. They attained wealth and we were in great distress. We were led in a band to a place where we could not make any headway . . .

When I think back to the time when we were free and had stags, deer, and buffalo, I feel very sad especially when I go to bed hungry.

Within hours of the first shots fired, the Lakota had won. General Custer and his battalion of 225 soldiers were dead; the only survivor was a horse named Comanche.

News of the Sioux victory stunned officials when it reached Washington, D.C., just as their centennial celebration ended after July 4, 1876. Within months, more soldiers occupied the plains and the Sioux fled north into British territory.

As a survivor of the Battle of Little Bighorn, Standing Bear toured Europe with Buffalo Bill Cody's Wild West Show. The highlight of the show was a re-enactment of the battle. While on tour, Standing Bear learned that his first wife and baby daughter were among the three hundred Lakota killed by U.S. soldiers at Wounded Knee.

A poster for Buffalo Bill's Wild West and Congress of Rough Riders of the World

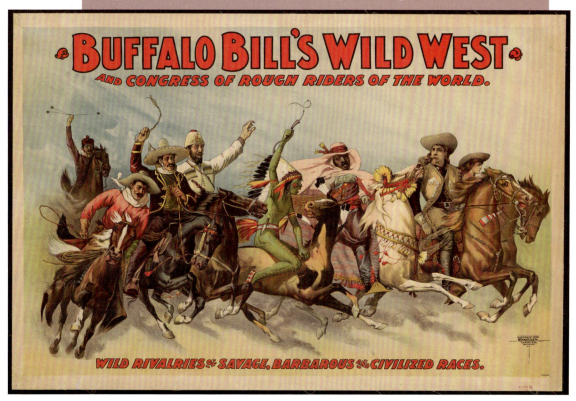

Dr. Charles Eastman
(1858–1939)

Dr. Charles Eastman, also known as Ohíye S'a, was a rare person because he had the skills to tell his story about his Sioux culture in English. He was the first Sioux person to receive a college education, so he didn't need anyone to translate his thoughts. He was a medical doctor who returned to his home community in 1890, just weeks before some of his fellow Sioux were massacred at Wounded Knee. He arrived on the scene to help the survivors. His first book, *Indian Boyhood* (1902), is his recollection of his carefree childhood on the open prairies in the last days of the buffalo. Then adult duties led him to medical school in Boston, Massachusetts, where he learned to be a healer for his people.

Standing Bear met his second wife, Louise, in Vienna, and she and her parents returned to South Dakota with him. Sometime in the 1930s, Standing Bear, who could not read or write, dictated his letter for Louise to write down. She translated his Sioux words into Old German, the language she knew best.

Ninety years later, Standing Bear's letter and a piece of his ledger art were found among papers that had been donated to a museum in Brampton, Ontario. They have now been returned to the Lakota community in South Dakota. The art may not be published because it shows sacred items from the Sun Dance, but the letter is a valuable way for us to get a clearer picture of what happened on that hot day in June by the banks of the Greasy Grass River.

Opposite: Statue of Chief Standing Bear at National Statuary Hall in Washington, D.C. His eyewitness account of what happened at Little Bighorn remains an accurate report of that event.

Wrangel Island party, 1922: (front row) Ada Blackjack (left) and Milton Galle (right); (back row) Fred Maurer, (left) and Lorne Knight (right); Allan Crawford is on the far left, pulling the string to operate the camera

Chapter 13

ADA BLACKJACK
Kept a Journal
Inupiaq, 1898–1983

Ada Blackjack grew up in the rowdy gold rush town of Nome, Alaska. Missionaries taught her enough English to study the Bible and to read and write at a Grade 3 level. She learned how to sew, keep house, and cook the food that Inuk seldom ate. What she didn't learn was any Inupiat knowledge of how to survive on the land. Yet Ada was a survivor, and she kept a journal to tell her story.

ADA BLACKJACK WAS ONLY sixteen when she married a brutal dog musher named Jack Blackjack. Together they had three children. Two of them died as babies.

Bennett, her surviving child, contracted tuberculosis. Medicine and doctors cost money and Ada had none. She couldn't bear the pain of losing another child, so she sent him to an orphanage where doctors and nurses would look after him for free. Ada swore she would find enough money to get care for him at home.

Ada was trudging home from a day of cleaning houses when the chief of police called out to her. He told her that an explorer named Vilhjalmur Stefansson was planning an expedition to claim Wrangel Island, a small island northeast of Siberia, for the British Empire. Four young men—Allan Crawford, Fred Maurer, Lorne Knight, and Milton Galle—made up the team. The expedition needed someone to sew up tears in heavy fur clothing. A rip could mean freezing to death in the frigid arctic air. The police chief had heard that Ada was a good seamstress. There might be a job for her.

Ada had big misgivings. She worried about going off into the wilderness with the men. Besides, she was a city girl who knew nothing of living on the land. Worse, she was afraid of being eaten alive by a polar bear. She consulted a shaman. *That is your choice,* he told her, *but death and danger will surround you.*

Ada chose to join the expedition anyway. After all, she would only be gone for a year. Stefansson had promised to hire more Inupiat for his team. Her salary was $50 a month—well above most jobs at the time and enough to bring Bennett home.

Ada Blackjack with her son, Bennett, in 1923

On September 9, 1921, with six months of supplies, assurances that there would be plenty of game to hunt and guarantees that a boat would meet them a year later, Ada, the explorers, and a kitten named Victoria (Vic) set sail on the *Silver Wave.* To her dismay, no Inupiat, with all their hunting and camping skills, were on the expedition.

When they arrived on barren, windy Wrangel Island, they found a place of frozen tundra, gray mountains, and dark gravel beaches. Ada watched the *Silver Wave* sail away while the four men unfurled the British flag and claimed the island for England.

At first things weren't bad. Crawford, Maurer, Knight, and Galle made notes in their journals about the animals they saw and the weather conditions. Their writing captured Ada's interest, but Galle warned her never to touch his typewriter.

Months passed. The days grew short, and the men often came back empty-handed from hunting. When summer came, they began to watch for the relief ship's return. Instead, their concern grew as the pack ice closed in, making the sea impossible. They didn't know that the ship, called the *Teddy Bear,* had tried to get them, but the thick ice surrounding the island forced it to turn back. They were facing a hungry winter, with little food and no ammunition for hunting.

As 1923 began, they were close to starvation and Knight was deathly ill. Crawford, Mauer, and Galle left him with Ada and set out with five dogs across the ice toward Siberia in search of help. They were never seen again.

Knight had scurvy, caused by a lack of vitamin C. He grew thin. His teeth were loose in his mouth. He was bleeding internally and too exhausted to move. One morning Ada woke up to the sound of dripping. She thought it was rain. Instead, she learned Knight's nose was bleeding profusely.

Now Ada had to keep them both alive. Despite her terror of polar bears, she left

Ada Blackjack removing blubber from a sealskin during the expedition to Wrangel Island the tent every day to look for food. She taught herself to shoot and to trap foxes so she could make broth from their meat. Knight couldn't chew anymore.

Throughout the expedition, Ada had watched the men record everything in their notebooks, but she had never set her own thoughts down on paper. She began to keep a journal. At first, she wrote about the kinds of things the men had thought were important, all about the foxes she caught and what the weather was like, and whether her head or stomach hurt.

She realized that Knight was not getting better, and that she might die too. Now she felt an urgent need to write her will for the sake of her son. "If anything happen to me and my death is known, there is black stirp for Bennett school book bag, for my only son. I wish if you please take everything to Bennett that is belong to me. I don't know how much I would be glad to get home to folks."

For six months Ada attended to Knight. She did everything for him while he took out his fright and pain on her, criticizing her constantly. She let his words rain on her, but in her diary, she wrote, "He never stop and think how much its hard for women to take four mans place, to woodwork and to hund [hunt] for something to eat for him and do waiting to his bed and take the shiad [shit] out for him."

Galle had warned Ada not to use his typewriter. But he was gone, so how could he stop her now? Despite his nagging, Knight was her only human companion, and he was close to death. She wanted to leave a record for Galle and for Knight's family. She typed:

Dear Galle,

I didn't know I will have very important writing to do. You well forgive me wouldn't you. Just before you left I've told you I wouldn't write with your typewriter. So I made up my mine I'll write a few words, in case some happen to me, because Mr. Knight he hardly know what he's talking about I guess he is going die he looks pretty bad. I hope I'll see you when you read letter. Well, if nothing happen to me I'll see you. The reason why I write this important notice I have to go out seal hunding with the rifle. Of course Knight wouldn't eat any meat he always say he's got sore throad. That's about all I well say in this notice I write. I may write some more times if nothing happen to me in few days.

With lots of best regards to your self from me
Yours truly
Mrs. Ada B. Jack

On June 10 she wrote:

This very important in case I happen to die or some body find out that I was dead I want Mrs. Rita McCafferty take care of my son Bennett. I don't want his father Black Jack to take him on a count of stepmother not for my boy. My sister Rita is just as good his on mother I know she love Bennett just please let this know to the judge. If I got any money coming from boss of this company if $1,200 give my mother Mrs. Ototook $200 if it is only $600 give her $100 rest of it for my son. And let Rita have enough money to support Bennett.

When Knight died, she sat down at the typewriter:

Wrangel Island
June 23, 1923

The daid [date] of Mr. Knight's death He died on June 23rd I don't know what time he die though Anyway I write the daid. Just to let Mr. Stefansson know what month he died and what daid of the month.
writen by Mrs. Ada B. Jack

The next morning, she didn't have the heart—or the strength—to move his body from his sleeping bag so she left him where he was. Except for Vic the cat, she was alone against the Arctic. She fixed up a new home in the storage tent. She made a stove out of empty kerosene tins. She built a sleeping platform from driftwood. And every morning before she set out to hunt, she typed a note about where she had gone, in case the three men returned:

> *June 26th I'm going to take a walk to the smale Island. I saw two Polar bears going in shore from the ice way over west of the camp. It's four oclock now. I write down when I saw them. I don't know what I'm going to do I they come to the camp. Well, God knows.*

On August 20, Ada dreamed of a ship, but when she woke all she saw was dense fog. Outside she heard a strange rumbling noise. *It must be a walrus,* she thought. She picked up her field glasses and climbed up the ladder to her platform. She peered through the fog. Then she saw a white man and some Inupiat men in a skin boat. She scrambled down and waded into the water, hoping that Crawford, Maurer, or Galle had returned.

It was a stranger, Harold Noice. He brought her onboard the *Donaldson*, gave her hot coffee, and peppered her with questions, especially about Lorne Knight's death. Eventually he let her go back to the

Ada Blackjack standing by the main tent in the camp in late autumn

shed to gather her belongings and Vic.

Ada returned from Wrangel Island to a media storm. It was an ordeal for a quiet, shy person. All she wanted was to be with Bennett and her sister Rita. She couldn't walk down the street without people staring at her. She heard cruel rumors—that she refused to work on the island; that she had been hired for sex; that she was too interested in men and drink. Worst of all, people claimed that she had not taken care of Knight and that he had starved to death while she grew fat on ducks and foxes. The journal was her weapon against the rumors.

Eventually Ada got recognition for her heroism. She didn't think of

Ada Blackjack on board the *Donaldson* after she was rescued by Harold Noice

Ada Blackjack at the grave of Lorne Knight

herself as heroic. All she had wanted was to get home to her boy. Mostly, she wanted to forget Wrangel Island.

Though Ada reunited with Bennett and had another son named Billy, grief, poverty, and the nightmares never left her. In 1973, in a rare interview, she said that when she heard the howling of the dogs beneath the Arctic skies, she knew they were singing for those lost souls haunting the tundra.

Bennett was in poor health all his life. He died in 1972. Ada Blackjack lived another ten years and died peacefully at her home in Palmer, Alaska, at age eighty-five. Thanks to her son Billy's efforts, the Alaska Legislature officially honored her on June 16, 1983, as a true and courageous hero.

When people called Ada brave, she would say, "Brave? I don't know about that. But I would never give up hope while I'm still alive." Ada's journal tells the real story. She was resourceful, caring, and incredibly brave.

A newspaper article from February 27, 1924, about Ada Blackjack and her son, Bennett

Opposite: A page from Ada Blackjack's journal

one day I went out again, it was the 4th of July (I made a calendar out of typewriting paper cut into small pieces - I had one for 1922 but I had to make my own 1923 calendar which I still have in my trunk). When I went to get my third seal I was crawling and crawling along on my stomach to get up close enough to shoot it and I was just ready to aim when it moved so that a large ice cake extended in front or between me and the seal. So I was moving around to get a better aim, and I had my finger on the hammer, and in moving I must have pulled it down and BANG! went the gun and down went the seal into the water and I didn't get any meat. I thought, well, I had my 4th of July celebration anyway.

The beach was only a few yards from the back of my tent. The third seal I got I went out and about two hundred yards out from the beach on the ice was a seal, so I went out to take a shot at it and I got this one. It was so far out that I knew that I couldn't get it to the tent without something to help me. So I went back to the tent and got a poling line for seal and then started after my seal. I was nearly to it when I looked up and saw something that looked just like a yellow ball coming towards me. Finally I realized it was a polar bear and I was four hundred yards from my tent. I turned and ran just as hard as I could until I got to my tent. I was just about ready to faint when I got there, too. I had built a high raft at the back of my tent and I climbed up onto this and took my field glasses and watched the bear and her young one eat my seal, at least I thought she was anyway. It finally got dark and foggy so I decided I had better not take a chance and go after it that night so I waited until the next morning. I went out and took a look but my seal was gone, all that was left was a few blood marks. The old mother bear and her young later came up to about one hundred and fifty yards from the tent.

One day just after I had cleaned my second seal I heard a noise just like a dog outside of my door and I looked out the door and about fifteen feet from the tent was a big bear and a young one. I was very scared but I took my rifle and thought I would take a chance. I knew if I just hit them in the foot or some place where it would only injure them a little they would come after me, so I fired over their heads and they turned and ran a little ways and turned and looked as if they would come back, so I fired five more shots at them and they ran away for good then.

One morning after I had built a fire I opened the door and I found a large polar bear track right in the door way and I went out and looked and he had been all around the tent. I had a twenty-five pound lard tin of oil outside of my tent and about three days after the first bear had been there another bear came one night and ate all of that tin of oil. I think it was only one for the tracks all looked the same size.

Not very long after that the boat came. It was one evening about the 19th of August. I was making my lunch or supper. I heard a funny noise like a boat whistle but thought it was a duck or something. It was foggy and I couldn't see so I didn't think any more about it until the next morning. I took my book after supper, for I couldn't go to sleep until I had read a while, then I went to sleep. The next morning about six o'clock I heard that same noise again and it sounded more like a boat whistle this time so I grabbed my field glasses and went out on top of my raft, and sure enough there was a boat and the master and the people were walking around on the beach. I had only home tea for breakfast that morning, for I watched the boat to see if they were going to come up to my camp. I thought it might be just a whale boat. I didn't know what to do,

Weaving is one of the Indigenous crafts, part of craftivism as done by weaver and graphic designer Debra Sparrow.

PART 5

the real story. She was incredibly brave, resourceful, caring, and

Our Hands Tell Our Story

Stories can be sewn into skirts, or beaded on a cuff, or mixed into a recipe in a cookbook. In the hands of a craftivist, anything is possible. In 2003, craftspeople invented a new word, *craftivism*, to describe how people were combining traditional crafts with activism. Craftivists are artists around the world who use their skills to make statements about social and political justice. Agnes Woodward makes ribbon skirts that tell the story of missing and murdered Indigenous girls and women. Elias Jade Not Afraid makes spectacular beaded art, showing us that Indigenous culture is always evolving. The I-Collective is on a mission to reclaim customary food ways with an online cookbook.

Agnes Yellow Bear's ribbon skirts hanging on trees

Chapter 14

AGNES YELLOW BEAR
Stitches Her Story
Plains Cree, Kawactoose First Nation, b. 1982

Ribbon skirts tell a different story for every person who sews one or wears one. They are a way to show the past, share dreams, and express Indigenous pride. Agnes Yellow Bear sewed a ribbon skirt that has become part of history.

PART 5 | Our Hands Tell Our Story

109

When a woman walks into a room wearing a ribbon skirt, everyone takes notice. She's like a walking story.

—Agnes Yellow Bear, "What the Ribbon Skirt Means to Agnes Yellow Bear"

AGNES WAS NERVOUS. SHE HAD a big secret. "I had so much fear that it wasn't real, or it wasn't going to really happen," she said. "I didn't want to get my hopes up for something so powerful." The secret was out the day that Deb Haaland (Laguna Pueblo) was sworn in as U.S. Secretary of the Interior. Haaland wore a long blue skirt adorned with rainbow-colored ribbons, appliqué butterflies and stars, and a cornstalk to represent the Laguna Pueblo tribe in New Mexico. Agnes Yellow Bear could finally tell her secret. She had made the ribbon skirt for Deb Haaland to wear as she became the first Indigenous American to hold a cabinet post.

When European traders brought silk ribbons to North America around 1611, Mi'kmaw women used them to sew ribbon appliqués onto their skirts. The ribbons proved to be so popular that whenever traders traveled on the Great

Deb Haaland being sworn in as the interior secretary in March, 2021, wearing one of Agnes Yellow Bear's ribbon skirts

Lakes, the Prairies, and to the North, they always had silk ribbon with them.

The earliest needleworkers sewed layers of ribbons on cloth, replacing the painted lines that had decorated clothes and blankets. Sewing cloth rather than animal hides gave women freedom to create intricate patterns that reflected their own unique style.

A ribbon skirt is a basic A-line shape, with layers of ribbon, mostly silk-satin, sewn onto it. Ribbon skirts are more than fashion pieces; they express an identity. Skirts are worn in traditional ceremonies, in political protests, and even in the U.S. Congress. Every ribbon skirt is a story of revival and resilience.

Agnes Yellow Bear had a difficult family history. Her father endured years in residential school, and her mother lost her family in the Sixties Scoop. In 1982, the year Agnes was born, her aunt Eleanor (Laney) Ewenin was murdered on the outskirts of Calgary. Racism made Agnes ashamed of her Plains Cree roots. She once told a journalist on CBC Radio how she struggled with a sense of "constant disappointment. That constant feeling of injustice. That constant feeling of feeling defeated."

Instead of Native pride, she felt shame when she wore a ribbon skirt. "My family jokes about having to wrestle me into a skirt because I hated it so much, and the only reason I hated it was because I carried so much shame from racism."

In 2005 she wore a ribbon skirt as part of her ceremonial regalia. Then came a turning point. After the ceremony, she was about to change out of her ribbon skirt to enter a store. Suddenly, she realized that by doing so, she was declaring her shame of her identity. Keeping her ribbon skirt on was her statement of liberation. Today, Agnes wears her ribbon skirts proudly.

Agnes started sewing because her children needed powwow outfits, and she couldn't afford to have someone else make them. She taught herself to sew and soon people started asking her to create skirts for them.

Some people object to the modern style they see in some ribbon skirt designs, but each one is a personal statement. They are often whimsical and may include design elements such as cartoon characters. People have asked Agnes to make skirts adorned with their name, their tribe, and even a tribute to Yoda from *Star Wars*.

Agnes's skirts also carry important messages. She made a skirt to represent her aunt who was murdered, and to give her mother comfort. Since then, she's made over three hundred ribbon skirts for family members of missing and murdered women and girls.

"Almost every skirt I do tells a story. When Indigenous women or Two Spirit people order a ribbon skirt it's with a deep purpose and I hear stories of survival, resilience, accomplishments. Sometimes it's to make a political statement, like the Indigenous children whose remains have been found at residential schools in Canada or the U.S. More than a political statement, it's a representation of our connection to each other."

Agnes Yellow Bear wearing one of her ribbon dresses

Chapter 15

ELIAS JADE NOT AFRAID
Beads His Story
Apsaalooke, b. 1991

Worried that he'd be bullied, at first Elias Jade Not Afraid didn't tell anybody about his passion for beading. After all, beading was something girls did. But as he became skilled, Elias realized that he could tell a story with beads.

Left: Beaded flower panel by Elias Jade Not Afraid

SINCE ANCIENT TIMES, PEOPLE have adorned themselves and their clothes with beads. Archaeologists have found them laboriously shaped from all kinds of natural materials: shells and pearls; stone, pottery, and metals; bones, teeth, claws, hooves, and horns; nuts, seeds, and even fossilized plant stems.

Nearly four thousand years ago, members of the shíshálh Nation buried their chief in a ceremonial garment covered in over 350,000 small stone beads. An archaeologist tried to make just one of the beads with the same tools and techniques the shíshálh had used. A single bead took thirteen minutes to

Examples of the elaborate beadwork done by Elias Jade Not Afraid

make. Multiply that by 350,000! Hundreds of artists must have worked to make a garment splendid enough for the chief to wear in the afterlife.

When European settlers arrived on our shores, they brought glass beads from Italy with them. Indigenous people were eager to trade furs for the glass beads. They came in gorgeous colors. They were tiny, so one person could carry hundreds of them. The Europeans' metal needles, textiles, and thread made them easy to use. Glass beads were soon so popular that they even substituted for money.

Elias Jade Not Afraid learned how to bead when he was growing up on the Crow Reservation in Lodge Grass, Montana. Although his great-grandmother, Joy Yellowtail, died before he was born, he says that she was his biggest influence. When he was twelve, he was living in her old house. There wasn't much to do in the bitter cold of a Montana winter, and he was bored. One day, he discovered a large cedar trunk. Inside was his grandmother's beadwork.

Elias didn't grow up knowing his people's language or traditions, so he didn't know how important beads were. He just thought they were beautiful. Over and over, he took apart pieces of her beadwork and put them back together until he realized he had learned to bead.

From the beginning, beading meant a lot to him. "I grew up having a rough childhood. With living in the country, I had very little to do, so I channeled all of my emotions while growing up into my work. I would bead if I was upset, hurt, sad, and even when happy."

Elias kept his skill a secret until his senior year in high school. He worried people would make fun of him because beading was thought of as women's work. Beading gave Elias the confidence to stop caring what people thought of him. He beaded at school and realized that the

Beadwork medallion signifying the artist's name

other kids thought it was cool. Around the same time, he came out as gay.

Elias broke gender stereotypes with his beading and defied expectations of what beadwork was supposed to look like. Traditional Crow beading had specific colors and designs. Elias ignored the rules: his fifth project was a skull medallion, certainly not a traditional design.

At first, he didn't think that he could make a living by beading. He sold a few small pieces, but at the time, Elias had an addiction, and what money he earned he spent on drugs. He realized that addiction meant he was wasting his life. He says beading gave him the strength to get sober, and to stay that way.

Elias wanted to learn everything he could about the history of his art. He traveled to Chicago to study the Field Museum's collection of beadworks and learn the ancient styles that nobody used anymore. He figured out how to copy beadwork techniques no longer practiced. He put together digital tutorials to teach others and to ensure these methods remain vibrant. Now his work is on display in museums.

Elias continues to take chances. He's done skull medallions with glass and 24-karat gold cut beads; he's also done a fully beaded Crow-style belt lined with stingray and lambskin. His bestsellers are Kevlar cuffs. They combine traditional Crow design with the punk look.

Today beadwork can adorn everything from patches on jeans to jewelry and traditional regalia worn in ceremony and at powwows. As Elias says:

"Beadwork is vital for our tribe's survival in these modern times to keep our culture and traditions alive."

It does this, he says, "by not only teaching others how to bead but to continue and push boundaries and limits by evolving the designs and patterns like our ancestors did, with both floral and geometric designs in their beadwork, and understanding what certain designs and colors mean to Crow people. I try to do this by making beadwork interesting to the younger tribal members by using bright and vibrant colors or by beading something they might find 'cool' like beaded snakes."

The story he tells in beadwork is clear. "The art of Native American beadwork is still here, just as we are," he says. "Now watch us evolve into something our ancestors never thought possible."

"Life After Death" cradle board purchased by the Metropolitan Museum of Art in New York City

Nuchu and Dinè youth foraging for traditional Indigenous foods such as chanterelles, wild onions, valerian, and arnica

Chapter 16

THE I-COLLECTIVE
Tells the Story with Food
Various

Indigenous, inspired, innovative, independent. Those ideas guide the I-Collective, which is a group of Indigenous cooks, chefs, seed keepers, educators, activists, and advocates. Their multimedia cookbook, *A Gathering Basket*, reveals traditional Indigenous knowledge about old-style foodways using modern technology.

Above: Karlos Baca foraging for food

PART 5 | Our Hands Tell Our Story

THREE FRIENDS FOUNDED THE I-Collective in 2017. Since then, it has grown to include over twenty members from across North America. Among them are citizens of the Choctaw, Frog Lake Cree, Pawnee/Athabaskan, and other nations. They are determined to keep Indigenous knowledge about country food, sea food, and agricultural practices alive.

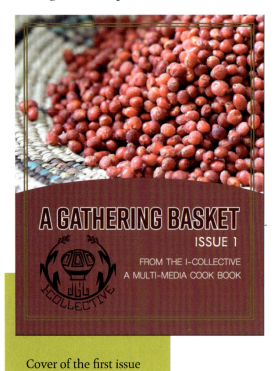

Cover of the first issue of *A Gathering Basket*

The I-Collective launched its multimedia publication *A Gathering Basket* in 2021 to reclaim Indigenous food knowledge. It features digital issues, webinars, and videos. The visual storytelling is a way of respecting and preserving food traditions and culinary practices. After all, the best way of learning about food is by watching, doing, and eating.

Readers can learn about the history of traditional foods and how to prepare them, or learn about brand-new things to taste, such as sumac popsicles. Although it is designed for Indigenous people, the website is open to anyone who is interested in or curious about nature's food stuffs.

The second issue is a good example of what you can find in *A Gathering Basket*. The theme is the walleye, a delicious fish that's found around the Great Lakes. There's a video by an experienced fisherman

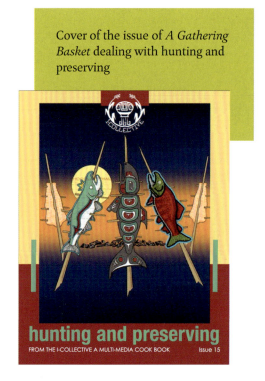

Cover of the issue of *A Gathering Basket* dealing with hunting and preserving

named Tre'Shaun Neadeau (Makwa/Bear Clan) showing how to clean a walleye; a recipe for preparing the fish with a crust of toasted pepitas, sunflower seeds, corn meal, and sumac; and an article by Vernon DeFoe (Anishinaabe), who developed the recipe.

Each issue links food to history. In the issue on walleye there is also an article and a video about fishing rights, and viewers can read about the Walleye Wars of 1985–1991. Readers learn about how, beginning around the 1950s, the Bad River Tribe fought for their treaty rights to hunt and fish for food regardless of the season. They faced hostile officers who confiscated their fish, game, and the wild rice they had collected, along with their fishing spears, nets, and rifles. Some tribal members were even sent to prison. They discovered that following the traditions of their ancestors meant they first had to be treated like criminals.

We also learn that good things have come from the conflict. Today, the Great Lakes Indian Fish & Wildlife Commission protects the reservation ecosystems and is a leading caretaker of the land and water.

A useful feature of *A Gathering Basket* is advice on how to find traditional ingredients. One of the biggest challenges of practicing Indigenous food ways is finding wild game and certain kinds of corn, beans, or chilies, since they aren't usually mass produced. Also, some recipes call for food items that take a lot of time to prepare. For instance, acorn flour requires harvesting thousands of acorns, opening them by hand, and blanching them before grinding them into powder. Experts need huge amounts of technical skill, time, and energy just to produce one pound. Knowing where to buy ready-made acorn flour is helpful.

A Gathering Basket tells an important story: respect for the natural world and its plants and animals is in every issue. It's the story of all Traditional Knowledge. The food we eat is a gift to be treated with respect.

Cooking using local ingredients from the streams, rivers, and forests to revitalize healthy Indigenous cuisine

Our Stories Go On

Eldon Yellowhorn poses with a group of Maya dancers in Chiapas, Mexico.

Afterword by
ELDON YELLOWHORN

Piikani Nation

FOR MY PIIKANI ANCESTORS, winter was the season for storytelling. Settling beside a warm fire in a tipi, tellers recalled the stories of ancient times. Stories were magic. They helped to push back the darkness on a long, cold night. Like the dreams that fill our sleep, stories unleash adventure, mystery, and fantasy on our imagination.

Stories changed when Europeans introduced their alphabet. Writing was a foreign custom that Indigenous people accepted because it was a new way to communicate with each other. They also discovered that writing could easily spread misinformation as truth. So, they used their words to tell the world about themselves, their nations, and their cultures. For example, after Elias Boudinot converted to Christianity, he found his voice by writing in English to reach out to the settlers in his Cherokee homeland. Pauline Johnson

Eldon Yellowhorn visits L'Anse aux Meadows, where the Viking settlement was discovered. Behind him is the Strait of Belle Isle, Newfoundland and Labrador.

expressed her voice through the poetry she recited in dramatic performances on stage, in poems of Haudenosaunee (Six Nations) history, and in prose drawn from the Squamish legends that Joe and Mary Capilano told her. Ella Cara Deloria, whose voice of authority came from her academic research, composed historical fiction based on Sioux culture and filled with characters who used the objects she studied. These writers were storytellers who came from different times and circumstances, but they shared a common desire to correct the distorted views they read about their people.

Stories never lost their magic even though the printing press replaced the storyteller and reading replaced listening. No matter how they are told, stories keep their entertainment value because all audiences want to be entertained. Today, storytelling is no longer a seasonal activity because the whole year is story time! Creative writing is a profession rather than a pastime, but stories can still transport the reader to another reality. Authors of prose, poetry, graphic novels, video games, or TV shows imagine situations for the characters they write into existence. Fans of these works also care about these fictional personalities when they conjure in their mind the realm where the action unfolds. It is a private place they can enter just by opening a book.

People are compelled to make up stories. That was true for our ancestors; it is true today; and it will be true for future writers. There will always be a demand from spectators who listen to satellite radio, read e-books, or stream their favorite television show. Tomorrow, readers will have new technology and new media that will affect the way they relate to authors, books, and stories. Indigenous writers will still entertain audiences and connect with readers using words to unravel a good plot. They will compose new stories about the things that matter to them and invite readers to inhabit the worlds they create.

Literacy is the ability to read and write. In ancient America only the Maya in Mexico invented writing. After the Spanish conquest, Franciscan priests such as Diego de Landa burned their libraries and banned scribes from using their customary hieroglyphic writing. If they wanted to keep their jobs and communicate their stories, they had to learn the alphabet introduced by the Spanish. When they forgot the meanings behind those images in the books that were tossed into bonfires, the Maya lost an important connection to their history.

Indigenous people across North America had their own traditions of picture writing, but nobody uses them anymore, and the only examples persist on stone outcrops or in museums. Writing for the modern world was a skill that few Indigenous people possessed or had the opportunity to learn. Therefore, they always appeared as characters in someone else's story. Inevitably they were typecast as villains who brought danger to peaceful settlers. Back then most people had no occasion to put pen to paper, and if they had to compose a letter, they got someone to write for them. Those who embraced literacy were the innovators who seized the written word to set their thoughts on paper and get them published. We can be grateful that they left us their memoirs because we get a glimpse of their world and their struggles. Not everyone shared that goal. Since literacy arrived with settlers, they used it to promote outrageous stereotypes that still appear in popular culture. Sometimes they even became the characters of their own fiction.

Stolen identity is not a modern problem. It has been around for ages. Readers and audiences expect an authentic voice from the author when they pick up a book or share a poem. They accept that the writer who shares their experience as a member of a specific community is speaking the truth. Usually for money and fame, some artists will create an identity and then become their own fictional character to advance their careers. Each false claim causes harm because the public begins to distrust the creative works produced by all Indigenous people, who then face greater obstacles in getting recognition for their poems, novels, and songs. Despite this backdrop of fake stardom and phony celebrities, the public still wants stories that are authentic, real, and original.

Stories were always important in our Oral Tradition, and we gave them an update with writing. Now storytelling is our shield against toxic beliefs. Modern Indigenous authors compose narratives that challenge such views, and their audiences find sympathetic portrayals of characters who encourage positive relations. As authors, we are capable of creative expressions in our own voice. However, we also invite story lovers everywhere to become entangled in our yarns. We write to share our narratives with the world and to recount the lives of our relations. We write because our stories are ours to tell.

Sources and Resources

Introduction
p. 8 (epigraph): Alter, Alexandra. "Tommy Orange's 'There There' Is a New Kind of American Epic." *New York Times*, May 31, 2018. https://www.nytimes.com/2018/05/31/books/tommy-orange-there-there-native-american.html.

Chapter 1: Gaspar Antonio Chi
p. 14 (the scribe Tizmin): Roys, Ralph L., trans. *The Book of Chilam Balam of Chumayel.* Norman: University of Oklahoma Press, 1967. Originally published 1933.

p. 16 (Marisol Ceh Moo): Ceh Moo, Marisol. *X-Teya, u puksi'ik'al koolel [Teya, The Heart of a Woman]*. Mexico City: CONACULTA, 2008.

Chapter 2: Sequoyah
Foreman, Grant. *Sequoyah.* Norman: University of Oklahoma Press, 1938.

Summit, April. *Sequoyah and the Invention of the Cherokee Alphabet.* New York: Bloomsbury, 2012.

Chapter 3: Elias Boudinot
Gaines, Richard M. *The Cherokee.* Edina, MN: Abdo Publishing, 2000.

Perdue, Theda, ed. *Cherokee Editor: The Writings of Elias Boudinot.* Knoxville: University of Tennessee Press, 1983.

Chapter 4: Ella Cara Deloria
Deloria, Ella Cara. *Waterlily.* Lincoln: University of Nebraska Press, 1988.

King, Charles. *Gods of the Upper Air: How a Circle of Renegade Anthropologists Reinvented Race, Sex, and Gender in the Twentieth Century.* New York: Anchor Books, 2019.

p. 34 (Vine Deloria Jr.): Deloria, Vine Jr. *Custer Died for Your Sins: An Indian Manifesto.* Norman: University of Oklahoma Press, 1988. Originally published 1969.

p. 36 (*Walking Eagle News*): Fontaine, Tim. *Walking Eagle News.* 2017–2024. https://walkingeaglenews.com/.

Chapter 5: Pauline Johnson
Johnson, E. Pauline. *E. Pauline Johnson, Tekahionwake: Collected Poems and Selected Prose,* ed. Carole Gerson and Veronica Strong-Boag. Toronto: University of Toronto Press, 2002.

p. 43 ("A Cry from an Indian Wife"): Johnson, E. Pauline (Tekahionwake). *Flint and Feather.* Toronto: Musson Book Co., 1913.

p. 47 (story collections): Johnson, E. Pauline. *Legends of Vancouver,* 100th anniversary edition. Vancouver: Midtown Press, 2011; Shield, Alix, ed. *Legends of the Capilano* by E. Pauline Johnson (Tekahionwake)

Ella Cara Deloria

with Chief Joe Capilano (Sahp-luk) and Mary Agnes Capilano (Lixwelut). Winnipeg: University of Manitoba Press, 2023.

Chapter 6: Tommy Orange
Orange, Tommy. *There There*. London: Vintage, 2019.

p. 51 (writing process for *There There*): Orange, Tommy. "A Conversation with Tommy Orange." Interview by Amy Starcheski, February 16, 2022. Oral History Master of Arts program, Columbia University. Video, 1:20:44. https://youtu.be/WI09Ipyn8sc?si=RpodMiWSTXAol9S3.

p. 53 (review of *There There*): Leu, Chelsea. "'There There,' by Tommy Orange." *San Francisco Chronicle*, June 7, 2018. https://www.sfchronicle.com/books/article/There-There-by-Tommy-Orange-12974292.php; ("His goal is to keep telling stories"): Orange, Tommy. Interview by Evan Smith, December 6, 2018. *Overheard with Evan Smith,* season 9, episode 13. PBS. Video, 26:46. https://www.pbs.org/video/tommy-orange-ljuxkd/.

Chapter 7: Rita Joe
Joe, Rita. *Songs of Eskasoni*. Charlottetown, PE: Ragweed Press, 1988.

p. 56 (foster homes): Joe, Rita. *Song of Rita Joe: Autobiography of a Mi'kmaq Poet.* Charlottetown, PE: Ragweed Press, 1996; ("brainwashed"): Joe, Rita. Interview with Ian McNeil. CBC Radio, date unknown.

p. 58 (poems): Joe, Rita. *Poems of Rita Joe.* Halifax, NS: Abanaki Press, 1978.

Chapter 8: Marilyn Dumont
p. 61 (epigraph): Dumont, Marilyn. Interview with Jónína Kirton. *Room* 46, no. 2: *Ley Line*, 2023. https://roommagazine.com/interview-with-marilyn-dumont/.

Chapter 9: Jay Odjick
Odjick, Jay. Interview with Kathy Lowinger, 2023.

Keeptwo, Suzanne. "Creator of *Kagagi, the Raven* a Superhero in His Own Right." *Anishnabek News*, September 16, 2016. https://anishinabeknews.ca/2015/09/16/creator-of-kagagi-the-raven-a-superhero-in-his-own-right/.

Chapter 10: Beatriz and Catalina
Reséndez, Andrés. *The Other Slavery: The Uncovered Story of Indian Enslavement in America.* New York: First Mariner Books, 2016.

Van Deusen, Nancy E. *Global Indios: The Indigenous Struggle for Justice in Sixteenth-Century Spain.* Durham, NC: Duke University Press, 2015.

Van Deusen, Nancy E. "Seeing Indios in Sixteenth-Century Castile." *William and Mary Quarterly* 69, no. 2 (2012): 205–34.

Chapter 11: Shanawdithit
Mitchell, Alanna. "Amet*: Understanding the Beothuk." *Canadian Geographic*, April 14, 2021. https://canadiangeographic.ca/articles/amet-understanding-the-beothuk/.

Pestore, Ralph T. *Shanawdithit's People: The Archaeology of the Beothuks.* St. John's, NL: Atlantic Archaeology, 1992.

Chapter 12: Standing Bear

p. 90 ("We want no white men here"): Brown, Dee. *Bury My Heart at Wounded Knee: An Indian History of the American West.* New York: Holt, Rinehart & Winston, 1970.

pp. 91–92 (letter from Standing Bear): Region of Peel Archives. "'Your Friend, Standing Bear': Coming Together Through Repatriation." Peeling the Past blog, June 8, 2022. https://peelarchivesblog.com/2022/06/08/your-friend-standing-bear-coming-together-through-repatriation/.

p. 94 (Dr. Charles Eastman): Ohiyesa [Charles Eastman]. *Indian Boyhood.* Originally published 1902. Ebook #337, Project Gutenberg, 2008. https://www.gutenberg.org/files/337/337-h/337-h.htm.

Chapter 13: Ada Blackjack

Niven, Jennifer. *Ada Blackjack: A True Story of Survival in the Arctic.* New York: Hyperion, 2003.

Chapter 14: Agnes Yellow Bear

p. 110 (epigraph): Tate, Clark. "What the Ribbon Skirt Means to Agnes Woodward, Creator of Deb Haaland's Swearing in Ceremony Ensemble." Craft Industry Alliance, April 20, 2021. https://craftindustryalliance.org/what-the-ribbon-skirt-means-to-agnes-woodward-creator-of-deb-haalands-swearing-in-ceremony-ensemble/.

pp. 110, 112 (Deb Haaland and ribbon skirts): Adach, Kate. "Deb Haaland Wore a Ribbon Skirt to Her Swearing In Ceremony. Meet the Designer Who Created It." CBC Unreserved, May 31, 2021. https://www.cbc.ca/radio/unreserved/indigenous-fashion-the-politics-of-ribbon-skirts-runways-and-resilience-1.6034149/deb-haaland-wore-a-ribbon-skirt-to-her-swearing-in-ceremony-meet-the-designer-who-created-it-1.6047011.

Chapter 15: Elias Jade Not Afraid

p. 114 (shíshálh Nation burial): Pearce, Joanne. "Digitally Reconstructed Faces of 4,000-Year-Old shíshálh Family Revealed." *Canadian Geographic,* May 11, 2017. https://canadiangeographic.ca/articles/digitally-reconstructed-faces-of-4000-year-old-shishalh-family-revealed/; Mackie, Quentin. "Bead-Rich Human Burials in shíshálh Territory." *Northwest Coast Archaeology,* August 31, 2012. https://qmackie.com/2012/08/31/bead-rich-burials-in-shishalh-territory/.

pp. 115–16 (Elias Not Afraid): Thompson, Darren. "Bead Artist Elias Not Afraid." Powwows.com, July 12, 2016. https://www.powwows.com/feature-elias-not-afraid/; Allaire, Christian. "Meet 8 Indigenous Beaders Who Are Modernizing Their Craft." *Vogue,* April 24, 2019. https://www.vogue.com/vogueworld/article/indigenous-beadwork-instagram-artists-jewelry-accessories; Not Afraid, Elias. "Conversation with the Artist: Elias Jade Not Afraid." Interview, January 19, 2021. Museum of Beadwork. https://www.museumofbeadwork.org/blogs/news/conversation-with-the-artist-elias-jade-not-afraid.

Chapter 16: I-Collective

Krishna, Priya. "A New Cookbook by Indigenous People, for Indigenous People." *New York Times,* October 11, 2021. https://www.nytimes.com/2021/10/11/dining/indigenous-people-food-cookbook.html.

Yu, Ji-Yin. "'We're Family': How the I-Collective Is Bringing Indigenous People and Food Together." *Today,* January 13, 2022. https://www.today.com/food/people/i-collective-brings-indigenous-people-food-together-rcna128787.

Image Credits Continued

1: Memorial University of Newfoundland. Libraries. Centre for Newfoundland Studies; 5 Library and Archives Canada; 7 Library of Congress Prints and Photographs Division; 9 Courtesy of Marilyn Dumont; 10-11 Andrea Izzotti / Alamy Stock Photo; 12 david sanger photography / Alamy Stock Photo; 14 history_docu_photo / Alamy Stock Photo; 15 The Picture Art Collection / Alamy Stock Photo; 16 top Courtesy of Sol Ceh Moo; 16 bottom Photo © NPL - DeA Picture Library / Bridgeman Images; 17 Tozzer Library Special Collections, Harvard University, Cambridge; 18 "Land of My Heart" by Bill and Traci Rabbit. Acrylic on canvas. Commissioned by the Cherokee Nation; 19 Library of Congress Prints and Photographs Division; 20 North Wind Picture Archives / Alamy Stock Photo; 21 Danita Delimont / Alamy Stock Photo; 22-23 right Copyright Tara Rose Weston; 22-23 left From Edward Curtis: Re-Imagined by Haley Day Rains (Muscogee Creek Nation); 24 © Courtesy, American Antiquarian Society / Bridgeman Images; 25 Muriel Wright Collection, 21642.2, Oklahoma Historical Society; 26-27 U.S. National Park Service; 29 Courtesy of Cherokee Phoenix; 30 U.S. National Archives and Records Administration (NARA); 31 Courtesy of Philip Deloria; 32 IanDagnall Computing / Alamy Stock Photo; 33 U.S. National Archives and Records Administration (NARA); 34 Photo by Chris Richards. Courtesy of Philip Deloria; 35 Reproduced by permission of the University of Nebraska Press; 36 THE CANADIAN PRESS/John Woods; 37 bottom Courtesy of Philip Deloria; 37 top Courtesy of Philip Deloria; 38-39 left Liz Hafalia/San Francisco Chronicle via AP; 38-39 centre George Paul; 38-39 right Courtesy of Marilyn Dumont; 40 E. Pauline Johnson, Tekahionwake : collected poems and selected prose / introduced and edited by Carole Gerson and Veronica Strong-Boag; 41 Charles S. Cochran, photo, Vancouver Public Library 9430; 42 Brant Historical Society – Other #00563 – 946.7.2g; 43 Charles S. Cochran, photo, Vancouver Public Library 9429; 44 The Artchives / Alamy Stock Photo; 45 Agnes Etherington Art Centre; 46 Photo by Stuart Thomson /City of Vancouver Archives; 47 top British Columbia Historical Books Collection; 47 bottom City of Vancouver Archives; 48 © Gregory Johnston | Dreamstime.com; 49 Liz Hafalia/San Francisco Chronicle via AP; 51 There There by Tommy Orange. Permission granted by Penguin RandomHouse; 52 NICOLE BENGIVENO/The New York Times/Redux; 53 Roger Kisby/Redux; 54 William Berry / Alamy Stock Photo; 55 Photo by George Paul; 57 Nova Scotia Museum; 58 Joe, Rita (1978). Poems of Rita Joe. Halifax, N.S: Abanaki Press; 59 CP PHOTO/Stf; 60 Photo by Adam Scotti (PMO); 61 Courtesy of Marilyn Dumont; 62 The Pemmican Eaters by Marilyn Dumont. Reprinted by permission of ECW Press; 63 top Studio Notman / Library and Archives Canada / e003895129; 63 bottom Harvey J. Strong / Library and Archives Canada / Jean Riel fonds / e011156649; 64 Courtesy of Pris Lepine; 66-70 Courtesy of Jay Odjick; 71 Bear for Breakfast / Makwa kidji kijebà wìsiniyàn by Robert Munsch, illustrated by Jay Odjick. Reprinted with permission by Scholastic Canada; 72-73 The Stapleton Collection / Bridgeman Images; 74 Smith Archive / Alamy Stock Photo; 76 Bridgeman Images; 77 Leyes Nuevas, 1543, Biblioteca Digital Hispánica; 78-79 © MCD. Archivos Estatales (España) / © MCD. State Archives (Spain); 80 Bridgeman Images; 82 Memorial University of Newfoundland. Libraries. Centre for Newfoundland Studies; 83 Library and Archives Canada; 85 Memorial University of Newfoundland. Libraries. Centre for Newfoundland Studies; 86 Provincial Historic Sites, Department of Tourism, Culture, Arts and Recreation, Government of Newfoundland and Labrador. Artist/sculpto: Gerald Squires; 87 top Courtesy of The Rooms Provincial Archives Division (MG-100), St. John's, NL; 87 bottom Library and Archives Canada; 88 Edward S. Curtis, 1868-1952, photographer/Library of Congress Prints and Photographs Division; 89 National Anthropological Archives, Smithsonian Institution; 90 Logic Images / Alamy Stock Photo; 91, 93 Library of Congress Prints and Photographs Division; 94 Minnesota Historical Society; 95 Artist: Benjamin Victor/Architect of the Capitol; 96 From The adventure of Wrangel Island by Stefansson, Vilhjalmur, published London: J.Cape, 1925; 97 Wilfrid Laurier University Archives and Special Collections; 98, 104 Dartmouth Libraries; 99-103 From The adventure of Wrangel Island by Stefansson, Vilhjalmur, published London: J.Cape, 1925; 106-107 MOA Collection 3356/1. Photo by Alina Ilyasova. Museum of Anthropology at UBC, Vancouver, Canada; 108-109 Courtesy of Agnes Yellow Bear; 110 AP Photo/Alex Brandon; 112 Courtesy of Agnes Yellow Bear; 113 Courtesy of Elias Jade Not Afraid; 113 right Photo by Latoya Flowers; 114-115, 117 Courtesy of Elias Jade Not Afraid; 118 Courtesy of M. Karlos Baca 120-121 Courtesy of I-Collective; 119 Courtesy of M. Karlos Baca; 127 Courtesy of Philip Deloria; 129 Courtesy of Agnes Yellow Bear; 130 Muriel Wright Collection, 21642.2, Oklahoma Historical Society.

Rita Joe, "I Lost My Talk," from Song of Eskasoni. Copyright © 2007 by the Estate of Rita Joe. Reprinted by permission of the Estate of Rita Joe.

Collages by Chantal Jung:

1-9, 124-136: a close up of a green book cover © Heather Green, unsplash.com; 5: Labrador Tea © Henry Schneider; Woman believed to be Shanawdithit, Library and Archives Canada; Sea Thrift, © Seema Miah, unsplash.com; 6 Indian Blanket Flower © Saqib Iqbal Digital, unsplash.com; a couple white flowers © Anna Evans, unsplash.com; Potrait of Sequoyah © Library of Congress Prints and Photographs Division; 7 white and yellow flower in tilt shift lens © David Thielen, unsplash.com; Maple Leaf © olga safronova, unsplash.com; Potrait of Marilyn Dumont courtesy of Marilyn Dumont 127 Chicory © Raymond Eichelberger, unsplash.com; Pasque Flower © Nikolett Emmert, unsplash.com; Portrait of Ella Cara Deloria courtesy of Philip Deloria; 130: Red Lily © wirestock, freepik.com; Blue Flax © Sergey Semin, unsplash.com Portrait of Agnes Yellow Bear courtesy of Agnes Yellow Bear; 134: Indian Blanket Flower © Saqib Iqbal Digital, unsplash.com; a couple white flowers © Anna Evans, unsplash.com; Portrait of Elias Boudinot © Muriel Wright Collection, 21642.2.

Index

Note: *Italic* numbers indicate images

A
All rags now (Dumont), 65
A-Yo-Ka, 20

B
Bathurst, Henry, 84
Battle of Little Bighorn, 91–93
Battle of Seven Oaks, 65
beading, 113–14, *114*, *115*, *117*
    history of, 114–15
    as means of storytelling, 116
Bears for Breakfast (Munsch; illus. Odjick), 71, *71*
Beatriz
    enslavement of, 75, 76, 77
    lawsuit against Juan Cansino, 77–78, 81
    legacy of, 81
Benedict, Ruth, 32, 34
Beothuk, 84–86
Beothuk Institution, 84
Black Lodge (Tipi Sapa), 32
Blackflies (Munsch; illus. Odjick), 70
Blackjack, Ada, *97*, *98*, *103*, *104*
    eyewitness accounts of, 100, 101, 102, 104, *105*
    heroism of, 103–4
    letter to Milton Galle, 100–101
    Wrangle Island expedition, 98–102
Blackjack, Bennett, 98, 99, 100, 101, 104, *104*
Blackjack, Billy, 104
Blackjack, Jack, 98
Blind Man's Eyes (Joe), The, 59
Boas, Franz, 32–33, *32*
books/novels, 35, 50–53, 125, 126
Boudinot, Elias, 25
    belief in education, 26
    and *Cherokee Phoenix*, 27, 28
    journalistic legacy of, 29
    New Testament into Cherokee translation by, 26
Buffalo Bill Cody's Wild West Show, 93, *93*

C
Cansino, Juan, 77, 81
Capilano, Joe, 45, 46
Capilano, Mary, 46
Catalina
    branding of, 77, 78
    enslavement of, 75
    lawsuit against Juan Cansino, 81
    legacy of, 81
Ceh Moo, Marisol, 16
Cherokee language and storytelling, 19–21
Cherokee National Council, 25, 26, 27, 28
Cherokee Phoenix, 24, 25, 27, 29, *29*
Chilam Balam, 14
Columbus, Christopher, 76
comics/graphic novels, 67, 68–71, 125
conquistadors, 14
Cormack, William Epps, 84, 86
counter mapping, 86
court records, 75, 77–78, *78*, 79, 81
craftivism, 107
crafts. *See* beading; ribbon skirts
Crawford, Allan, 98, 99
Crazy Horse, 90, 92
"Cry from an Indian Wife, A," (Johnson), 43
Custer, George Armstrong, 90, *90*, 92, 93
Custer Died for Your Sins (Deloria Jr.), 34
Custer's Last Stand, 89, 91–93

D
Dakota Way of Life The (Deloria), 35
de Landa, Diego, 15, 15–16
DeFoe, Vernon, 121
Deloria, Ella Cara (Anpetu Wast-win), *31*, *37*
    challenges of as writer, 34–35
    education of, 32
    letter to Ruth Benedict, 32, 35
    storytelling legacy of, 35
    study of the Lakota by, 33, 34
Deloria, Vine, Jr., 34, *34*

Demasduit, 84, 85–86
drawings/maps, 16–17, 21, 68–69, 85
Dumont, Gabriel, 62
Dumont, Jean-Baptiste, 63
Dumont, Marilyn, *39*, *61*
    challenging norms through poetry, 62, 64
    creative journey of, 61, 64
    education of, 63, 64
    Métis roots of, 62–63

E

Eastman, Charles (Ohíye S'a), 94, *94*
Edward VII, King, 45
Enote, Jim, 86
Ewenin, Eleanor (Laney), 111
eyewitness reports, 89, 91–93, 94, 97, 100–102, *105*

F

Flint and Feather (Johnson), 43
Fontaine, Tim, 36

G

Galle, Milton, 98, 99, 100
Gaspar Chi, Antonio
    and creation of Mayan/Spanish alphabet, 15–16
    family tree of, *17*
    resistance to Spanish settlers by, 16–17
    status and dress of, 14
    writing materials of, 16
Gathering Basket, A, *120*
    as important resource, 121
    multimedia cookbook, 119
    and visual storytelling, 120, 121
glyphs, 11, 13, 15
Grant, Cuthbert, 65

H

Haaland, Deb, 110, *110*
Howells, Emily, 42

I

"I Lost My Talk" (Joe), 56
Indian Boyhood (Eastman), 94
"Indian problem," 52
Indian Removal Act, 28
Indian Termination Policy, 52
Institute of American Indian Arts, 53

J

Jade Not Afraid, Elias, *113*
    importance of beading to, 115–16
    as teacher, 116
    as unconventional beading artist, 116
Joe, Frank, 57, 59
Joe, Rita, *38*, *55*, *59*
    healing through poetry, 55, 58
    as journalist, 58
    life on reserve, 57
    marriage to Frank, 57, 59
    songwriting of, 59
    storytelling legacy of, 59
Johnson, George, Chief, 42
Johnson, Pauline (Tekahionwake), *41*
    as performance artist, 41, 43, *43*
    as poet, 41, 42
    sexism and racism faced by, 44
    Stanley Park monument to, 47, *47*
    storytelling legacy of, 47
    travelling performances of, 43–44, 44–45, *45*, 46

K

Kagagi, the Raven, *66–67*, 67, 68, *68*, 71
Kagagi, the Raven (TV show), 68, 71
King Philip's War, 8
Knight, Lorne, 98, 99, 100

I

I-Collective, The *118–19*, *119*, 120
    See also *Gathering Basket, A*

L

Landback movement, 17
Legends of Vancouver (Johnson), 47, *47*
literacy, Indigenous, 125–26
Lopez, Gregorio, 78

M

Massasoit, Chief, 8
Maurer, Fred, 98, 99
Maya
    glyphic writing of, 15, *15*, 16–17
    Lost Empire of, 16
    modern lives and culture of, 16
    resistance to Christianity by, 15, *15*
    stories of, 13

Metacomet, Chief, 8, 51
Métis, 61, 62–63, 65
MicMac News, 58
Munsch, Robert, 70

N
Neadeau, Tre'Shaun, 120
Noice, Harold, 102
Nonosabut, Chief, 84
North-West Resistance of 1885, 65

O
Odjick, Jay, *67*
    and Algonquin language, 71
    determination to succeed, 69–70
    early love of comics, 68–69
    views on tradition and creativity, 71
Orange, Tommy, *8, 38*
    and ancestral trauma, 51–52
    on native writers, 8
    search for identity by, 50
    storytelling ideas behind *There There*, 51–53
    and symbolism, 51–52

P
Pemmican Eaters, The (Dumont), 62, *62*
Peyton, John, Jr., 84
pictographs, 15
picture books, 70
Plymouth Fort, 8
Poems of Rita Joe, 58, *58*
poetry, 41–43, 56, 58, 62, 63, 124
printing press, 26, 27, *27*

R
racism, 44, 50, 58, 64, 111
Really Good Brown Girl, A (Dumont), 62, 64
Reese, Buck Watie, 26
Reese, Oo-Watie and Susanna, 26
residential school(s), 56, 112
ribbon skirts, *108–9, 110*
    history of, 110–11
    as means of storytelling, 111–12
Riel, Louis, 65

S
sabak, 14
satirical journalism, 36
Sequoayah, *19*
    accused of witchcraft, 20
    activism of, 28
    interest in writing, 20
    invention of Cherokee syllabary by, 19, 20–21
    syllabary adopted by Cherokee, 25
    traditionalism of, 21
sexism, 44
Shawnadithit (Nancy April), *83, 86*
    drawings of, 85, *85, 87*
    mapmaking of, *82–83, 83,* 85
    and persecution of Beothuk, 84
Sitting Bull, 90, 91, 92
slavery, Spanish, 76–77
Song of Eskasoni (Joe), 59
songwriting, 59, 126
Speaking of Indians (Deloria), 35
Standing Bear, *89*
    in Buffalo Bill Cody's Wild West Show, 93
    letter about Custer's Last Stand, 91–93

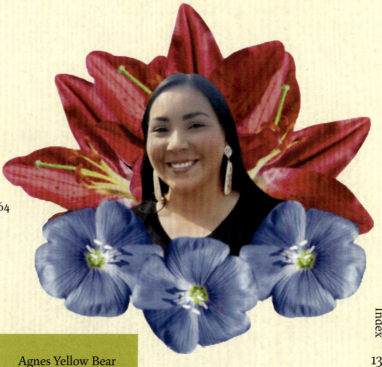

Agnes Yellow Bear

Index

133

as witness to history, 89, 94
Stefansson, Vilhjalmur, 98
story mapping, 86–87
storytelling
    Indigenous, 8, 126
    Indigenous evolution of, 124, 125
    and Oral Tradition, 126
    as part of everyday life, 125
    and stolen identity, 126
    and truth, 23, 124–25
syllabary, 19, 20–21, 25, 26, 27

T
"talking leaves," 25
Thanksgiving, 8–9
There There (Orange), 50, 51–53, *51*
Tizimin, 14
Traditional Knowledge, 15
Trail of Tears, 29
Treaty of New Echota, 28
Trudeau, Justin, *60*

U
urbanization of Indigenous peoples, 52

W
Walker, James R., 33
Walking Eagle News, 36
Walleye Wars, 121

Waterlily (Deloria), 35, *35*
webtoon, 70
White Wampum, The (Johnson), 44, *44*
Windigo, 68, 71
Woodward, Agnes, *109*, *112*
    feelings about ribbon skirts, 111
    ribbon skirt for U.S. secretary of the interior, 110
    as storyteller through ribbon skirts, 111–12
Worcester, Samuel, 26

X
Xiu Family Tree, *17*
X-Teya, u puksi'ik'al ko'olel (*Teya, Heart of a Woman*; Ceh Moo), 16

Y
Yellowhorn, Eldon, *124*
Yellowtail, Joy, 115

Elias Boudinot

on the Nov

ptain Buchan's visit in 1810-11 at the